DETOUR

My Brief but Amusing Career as a Bible Smuggler

Lloyd Sparks

iUniverse, Inc.
Bloomington

Detour
My Brief but Amusing Career as a Bible Smuggler

iUniverse books may be ordered through booksellers or by contacting:

iUniverse
1663 Liberty Drive
Bloomington, IN 47403
www.iuniverse.com
1-800-Authors (1-800-288-4677)

Because of the dynamic nature of the Internet, any web addresses or links contained in this book may have changed since publication and may no longer be valid. The views expressed in this work are solely those of the author and do not necessarily reflect the views of the publisher, and the publisher hereby disclaims any responsibility for them.

Any people depicted in stock imagery provided by Thinkstock are models, and such images are being used for illustrative purposes only.

Certain stock imagery © Thinkstock.

ISBN: 978-1-4620-6040-5 (sc)
ISBN: 978-1-4620-6041-2 (e)

Printed in the United States of America

iUniverse rev. date: 10/21/2011

For Liz

Contents

EAST GERMANY   1

POLAND   17

BULGARIA   41

GOING FULL TIME   73

HUNGARY   85

CZECHOSLOVAKIA   95

OPERATION HEAVY BOMBER   131

THE SOVIET UNION   151

A NIGHT AT DRACULA'S   207

A TIME FOR GOODBYES   231

POSTSCRIPT   239

EAST GERMANY

August, 1977

Dave set up another game, moving the center two pawns out two squares, as chess players bored with the first few moves often do. I followed in kind, halfway considering moving my knight instead just to show I was an independent thinker. But as a chess player I wasn't going to impress Dave. We had been playing off and on since the day before as I sat in the front seat next to him while he drove. We played, I in intense concentration, he glancing down at the board from time to time and moving a piece when it was his turn almost as an afterthought.

We were waiting in a long line at the East German border having just spent the night in Braunschweig in a boarding house run by three nuns. It was an often-used stopover for people like us coming from Holland and going in and out of the DDR, the German Democratic Republic, and we wanted to get the latest information that may concern us on our trip. I, a fledgling Bible smuggler, was not privy to the conversation that took place between the Mother Superior and our team leaders, Dave and Greg. At that point, it wouldn't have meant much to me anyway.

It was a warm and almost sunny August afternoon on the border between East and West Germany. It had been raining for the better part of the previous week and would continue to rain for the next two weeks of our adventure with the only other stretch of sunny weather being when we left the DDR and trundled home in our VW van, its windshield broken and engine grinding on the verge of collapse. We had purposely chosen to cross the border on a Friday afternoon because that was when traffic was heaviest. We needed to get lost in the crowd.

Dave continued his nonchalant chess game while his wife, Ruth, in the middle back seat knitted furiously. The longer we waited, the more intense the clickety-clack of the knitting needles became. She was doing her best to hide her tension in some wifely pastime. I'm not sure whether Ruth really liked to knit, but our brand of Christianity encouraged women to take up traditional women's activities like knitting and sewing. I once learned to knit from my aunt who told me she did it to take her mind off her worries. For me, it was only one more thing to worry about.

For Ruth, it wasn't working either.

Next to Ruth sat Susan. Susan was a teenager trying to find her calling in life. She, like me, had been chosen for this trip because of her three years of high school German. She had vague ideas about improving her German and then, having mastered it, moving on to another language. After that, if the Lord led, she might go into missionary work somewhere. I was in a position to give her some really valuable advice along those lines, having been in her situation about ten years earlier. A very wise man advised me to get a career, buy a house, marry and raise my family and then consider missionary work. Give back to charity only after you first have something to give. Career missionaries have no credibility and live a parasitic life of dependence upon others, constantly raising money to support themselves and their organizations, all the while feeling guilty if they ever spend a dime on their own pleasure. Susan was to make no use of my sage counsel for the same reason I had ignored some of the best advice I ever got: she didn't know what she really wanted out of life.

She would before the summer was over.

Neither Susan nor I were particularly nervous about our first Communist border crossing. Neither of us realized the danger we were in. As a matter of prudence, the mission had not told either of us that we were carrying anything illegal and Dave had just mentioned offhandedly that we had a few gifts for the believers we were going to meet both in East Germany and in Poland. We had volunteered knowing, indeed hoping, we would be smuggling Bibles into Communist countries just like Brother Andrew, whose organization, Open Doors, served as an umbrella for several smaller independent missions. But it looked from the start as though this would be nothing more than a chance to meet some believers in unregistered East German and Polish churches.

Greg was perspiring profusely. As he sat in the middle back seat next to the window, perspiration beaded on his forehead and ran in little rivulets down his face despite the constant mopping of his already soaked handkerchief. His shirt was wet front and back as well. He scanned the line of cars ahead of us and the activities of the border guards as we inched ahead. I had already made a military assessment of the area counting the personnel in uniform, noting their weapons and equipment, scouting the available cover and concealment as well as obstacles and fields of fire. Not that it served any real contingency plan. Just force of habit. Then I went back to playing chess.

Greg, never a soldier, saw the same area from an entirely different perspective. He was watching how the guards searched the vehicles. With German precision they systematically searched every car, looking under the hood, in the trunk, in the passenger compartment even taking out the seats, and opening every piece of luggage. They ran a mirror under every car and dipped a wire into every gas tank. Dogs (German shepherds, appropriately) sniffed around led by their canine olfactory curiosity. The guards were efficient and could do a car thoroughly in less than ten minutes. Every fourth vehicle was taken out of line and directed into what looked like some kind of a garage. Sometimes they didn't come out for almost an hour.

Greg let out a little grunt that sounded like a nasal, "uh-oh" which drew a glance from Dave.

"Nothing," Greg replied to the unspoken question.

"The garage," said Dave in a way that meant, "I know. I've been counting the cars, too."

We were one of the fourth cars and neither Dave nor Greg liked it. Ruth shifted gears into high.

"What do they do in the garage?" I asked.

"They take the cars apart and it takes a lot of time. I'd rather we got through the border as fast as possible and it could slow us up a bit," Dave explained. "Check."

"Huh?"

"My knight. You're in check."

"Oh, yeah."

Inside the garage, at that very moment, a West German was having a hard time explaining the forty kilograms of coffee he was trying to bring into the DDR. The roll of East German marks found taped behind the back seat didn't make things any easier. The coffee and the money would certainly be confiscated, but that would wait until the records were checked to see if Herr Whoever-he-was had been in trouble in the Worker's Paradise before.

And whether he had relatives.

I would find out later for myself that such a visit to the garage could slow up Bible smugglers by quite a bit. Months in some cases. Some people caught carrying in literature had been kept in prison for a very long time. It's not that it was a crime per se to bring in Bibles. All of the Eastern European Communist countries except Albania officially allowed the practice of religion and the ownership of Bibles. The governments even printed a few now and then. Religion, however, had no place in the Marxist-Leninist blueprint and was something to be discouraged. Moreover, a Bible on the black market carried a high price, and bringing them in could be construed as black marketeering. Then there was the catch-all crime used in the USSR and mimicked by the satellites of "anti-Soviet activity" under which virtually any human action could be tried in court and carried a potential death sentence.

But since we weren't carrying anything, I didn't see any reason to worry. I had personally packed everything we were carrying into the car at least twice already and there was definitely nothing of a suspicious nature in any of it. Greg was a little fat anyway. Maybe the sun through the window was just too warm for him.

The guard waved the fourth car ahead of us out of line and over to the garage line.

The Germans are an orderly people who form lines as naturally as baby ducks. Trying to buck the line is a social impropriety never tolerated without considerable resistance. So when the driver of a BMW crept up alongside the line and car by car pleaded to be let in (some story about having left something important at home) he was met with the sympathy ranging from cold shoulders to finger gestures.

Until he got to us. In Christian charity we graciously beckoned him into line ahead of us not even pretending to understand his story, but smiling in acknowledgement of his thanks, which were profuse. He had hardly begun to wedge his car into the opening gap in front of us when the guard blew two short blasts on his whistle and marched smartly toward our friend waving him into the garage line with a pop and snap that left no doubt as to his sincerity. No one bucked his line with impunity.

We all whispered prayers of thanks under our breath, perhaps Greg a little more fervently than the rest of us, and within an hour we were cruising smoothly through the DDR.

That evening we set up camp at an official but rather primitive campground. Dave, Greg and I set up the tents in the rain (men's work) while Ruth and Susan made us some hot food (women's work). Then we would go and make our first contact around dusk (spy work).

Nothing in my years of Army service in Military Intelligence and Special Forces had adequately prepared me for what was to follow. I knew what we were going to do and how to go about it properly. I also knew what to do should anything go wrong. My head was full of cover stories and contingency plans. I had faced much more dangerous situations than this before. Nevertheless, my hands shook and my heart beat in my throat. My breath came shallow and rapid.

As we passed the farmhouse for the third time, Dave said, "That's it, I'm sure. That has to be it."

It was the way he said "that has to be it" that told me that he wasn't a hundred percent certain. I could be walking into a fiasco.

Because my German was the best I was chosen to make initial contact. Since one does not want to attract the attention of the neighbors by knocking on doors, the proper way to approach an underground believer is to walk straight up to the door in the dead of night and walk right in unannounced. Thus the need to be absolutely certain that the house one is walking into is the right one.

And Dave wasn't certain.

But he was a cautious man and since, if one of us got into trouble the rest were as good as caught as well, I voiced no objection.

We pulled into the driveway, killed the engine and lights, and I went up to the front entrance. With a deep breath and a prayer, I turned the knob and pushed the door. It opened and I stepped into a living room filled with a German farming family.

There was no gasp of surprise, no shouting or mayhem. Just suddenly dawning smiles and, it seemed, recognition. Though we had never met before, they knew me and I instantly felt in my heart that I knew them, every one.

"Wilkommen, Bruder! Setzt Dich hin!" (Welcome brother! Have a seat!) they greeted me in the close "Du" form reserved for close friends and family. They knew I was a believer, and as such, family. I told them I had friends out in the car and Hans, the eldest son of the farmer went immediately out to invite them in and to show Dave where to park the van out of sight.

I experienced the witness of the Spirit, that knowledge and peace of being perfectly in God's plan with other believers. At that moment I knew I had found my calling. Working with the underground churches in Eastern Europe would be my life's work. I belonged. I was home.

There was commitment to their faith such as I had never seen. In America, one can shop for a church like one shops for clothes. Try one on and if it doesn't fit, just try another. In the underground churches, the choice was simple: believers or unbelievers. Neither the youth program, the choir, the pastor nor the building made any difference in why they went to church. To convert was to alter one's values and commitments permanently and there was no turning back. Such a situation rapidly eliminated anyone from the congregation who wasn't absolutely sure he or she wanted to be there. It was such a contrast to what I had grown up with. The opening line of the "Four Spiritual Laws" booklet so ubiquitous in America is, "God loves you and has a wonderful plan for your life." In Eastern Europe it would more likely have read, "God calls. Period."

The following day a secret youth meeting would be held that evening in the barn of the farmers. Before that we had some work to do. After a good night's sleep to the sweet music of rain on the tents we got up, had breakfast, and went on back to the farm. While Dave, Ruth and Susan passed the time in the house with the women and a baby, Greg and I went together with the van into the barn and bolted the door behind us. Then Greg very quietly and solemnly told me that what I was about to see I must never reveal to anyone, ever. It is only with the knowledge that the need for secrecy is long past and that the leaders of the mission have themselves revealed this much of the story that I recount it now.

Slowly and quietly Greg opened up the back of the van and took out the little red tool kit that rested under the back seat. Opening the tool kit he first removed a paint scraper and screwdriver. Then he began to gently tap around the great blue propane bottle that served as an alternative fuel supply for the van. The tone of the tap changed almost imperceptibly as he inched downward from the top and he knew he had found the right place. He spread a newspaper under the bottle and began to scrape ever so carefully with the scraper.

At first there was nothing to see but scratched paint and metal. Then after about ten minutes he reached a place where the metal had been cut. Next he found a screw flush with the metal plate, the slot filled with putty. He carefully chipped the putty out of the slot and picking up the screwdriver, began to remove the screw. It came out hard, as did the next three which held the metal plate secure. But when he removed the plate at last after a good hour's work, the dim light revealed that the propane tank was filled with literature.

We pulled out stacks and stacks of religious literature, mostly children's stories and some Christian adventure stories. Despite my amazement, I felt just a twinge of disappointment that there was not a single Bible in the stash. I had been told previously that German Bibles were not so rare in the DDR, but this kind of literature was. The authors of the books had had them translated into Eastern European languages at their own expense and donated the material to be smuggled in. They even paid for the expense of transporting the literature. Very noble.

Later, I would see the dilemma this arrangement presented to the mission. On the one hand, it was nice of people to cover the expense of bringing in literally thousands of pieces of Christian literature. On the other hand, that kind of material was rarely, if ever, requested by believers in the unregistered churches. I would make a systematic study in later years of the actual requests sent back and find that the most requested items were pastor study materials, followed by Bibles and children's material. Christian adventure stories were way down on the list. But the generosity of the authors in getting their own material also provided a means of transporting the more important items, and that explained the apparent incongruity.

After we removed the literature, we fastened and puttied the plate back into place and spray painted the propane bottle back to its normal blue color. We emerged from the barn, two and a half hours after having gone in, tired and grinning to ourselves like idiots. There was that post-stress rush, like after playing and winning a football game, and we were famished.

The German family was more than up to the task of feeding us. All the bounty of the farm was spread before us and we had a lunch fit for royalty. They chided us because we ate so little (!), but when I saw how the menfolk packed it away coming in as they were from a hard morning in the field, I could understand. Once I watched Doyle Kennedy break the world record in the dead lift, and even his awesome might barely impressed me as much as the men who shared the table with us. The 19-year-old Horst had arms as big as my thighs. Even his 9-month-old son seemed to eat more than I did. But Horst's father was known for slaughtering oxen with a single punch between the eyes. Looking at his massive fists spooning soup into his mouth, I doubted it not at all. I wondered how much the police dared to harass this family of gentle giants.

As the youth gathered that evening after sundown, we sat around in the big living room and exchanged introductions.

Then we sang songs, many of which they had written themselves or had been passed along to them from other such groups. There were guitars, always guitars. The Germans were a more stoic lot by nature, but loved music nevertheless and sang in that quiet, careful way that characterized every aspect of worship in the East. Secrecy was a part of their faith to which they had grown so accustomed that it came second nature, even by singing almost in whispers.

We shared testimonies with everyone and no one in particular translating. Most of them knew some English just as we all had a smattering of German. Then we brought out the literature. Horst laughed about how we had been in the barn so long that he thought we had either fallen asleep or were changing the van into a tank. They received the books with gratitude and we asked if there was literature on any particular topic we could try to find for them the next time we came. That was when the subject of the Charismatic Movement came up.

Greg was hopelessly in love with the Charismatic Movement. No one I've ever met believed in it, participated in it, and knew more about it than he did. He knew all the celebrities, read all the books and sang all the songs. He had the customary conversion from a life of sin, being saved from the depths of depravity, and received the baptism of the Holy Spirit with all the trimmings. He had apparently worked most of his younger years in the theater and movie industry claiming, truthfully I'm sure, to have met a number of famous actors, directors and producers. He had the stereotypical mannerisms and vocalisms of a flaming queen and at forty had never been married. I have to admit that I slept with one eye open for the first few nights we shared a pup tent, but we became good friends despite how little we had in common.

When Greg taught the Bible, he would open it to a verse that suited his fancy, start from there and never consult the pages again for hours. He spent the better part of two days teaching his philosophy on anything that came to mind, his ideas orbiting like planets around the Holy Trinity of charismatics: tongues, healing and prophecy. When asked a question or for clarification, he would get a far off gaze in his eyes, a detached and floating smile on his lips and slide right past the question with a God-will-explain-it-all-later comment of some kind.

Two days of intellectual torture made me realize that somebody should set this nonsense straight, but my own theology was so weak that I was in no position to do anything about it. The German believers, more than any other ethnic group I would meet, asked specific questions and wanted specific answers. Although I was fairly certain that Greg was a theological cripple, I had nothing better to offer. I made a mental note for when I got back home to get into some systematic theology. I particularly needed to sort out my position on prophecy, tongues and divine healing.

At that point in my life I had a fascination for alternative medicine and was hoping that I truly had the gift of healing. More than one Charismatic said that I had; I only needed to "develop" it. But the more I developed it, the more it eluded me.

One of the girls in the youth group had come down with

a fever and was in no shape to attend the meetings. Having just spent two days listening to a real Charismatic expound upon the necessary role miraculous healing plays in the life of the believer, it seemed natural that we should bring him over to pray for the lass. When the young people suggested it, Greg deftly dodged the responsibility. He stood up with great and solemn dignity and said that, although he had the gift of tongues and prophecy, the Lord had bestowed upon one of our number the gift of healing, and that gift belonged to me.

Denying it did no good; it looked like I was just being modest. Declining even to pray for the poor girl would be worse than impolite. So by default I found myself later that evening leading a stumbling group of disciples up a dark staircase in the house of the sick girl to her room, the blind leading the blind.

To my relief, as we entered the room the damp, sweaty, acrid smell of a fever freshly broken greeted me. She was over the illness, whatever it was, and needed to drink water and sleep. I could do nothing but introduce myself and suggest we offer thanks to the Almighty for healing her illness. I was particularly relieved.

The prayer was precisely one sentence long.

I was opening my eyes and starting to rise when Greg burst in with, "Oh Lord, we don't know why..." All his prayers seemed to start with that phrase. He prayed up the Spirit, down the demons, around the world about three times binding every evil entity in his path, claiming the healing, and pleading the blood. When he burst into a barrage of tongues, the girl peeked at me in alarm. I gave her my best reassuring nod.

Greg finished, winded and sweating, after about ten minutes. On the trip back to the campground he was full to bursting with joy and exhortations to trust God and believe in His power to perform miracles. Never doubt; only believe.

The next day we were to proceed on to Poland so we got back to the campground early enough to get a good night's sleep. There was no need to prepare supper as we had been fed very well by the Germans. Besides, it was raining and nobody wanted to bother with cooking anything anyway. I headed straight for my sleeping bag.

Greg, who shared the tent with me, came in about a half an hour later. He had a half hour ritual he performed every night regardless of the circumstances that started with taking all his medications and laxatives, brushing his teeth, flossing, cleaning his tongue, gargling, washing his face, changing into his pyjamas and slippers, performing his breathing exercises, reading his Bible, saying his prayers, and several more acts of importance understood only by himself.

"Sorry if I woke you, brother," he apologized, crawling in through the dripping flap. "I have to take a little more time than most people do to get ready for bed. Travelling as much as I do, I can't afford to let my personal hygiene slip even for a day."

If by that he meant that the rest of us were pigs, he may have had a point. By the end of the trip, we would all be calling dibs on the first hot shower as we neared the Dutch border. Greg, however, would be fresh as morning dew.

He explained to me that his idiocentricities were the reason he had never married. No girl would put up with such a man and he was too old to change his ways. That may have been true enough, but he was also dedicated to a profession that involved continual travel and no small amount of risk.

I drifted off to sleep wondering what I would be doing when I reached forty.

POLAND

"Dziekuje bardzo. Mmmph!" I said, thanking the young Polish border guard as he returned my passport and stifling a yelp of pain as Greg stamped my foot. We were standing at the passport control counter as they checked our documents and asked about the purpose of our trip to Poland and which cities we intended to visit.

"Czy wy mowy po polsku?" he asked me.

"Nein!" Greg answered for me in one of the five or six German words he knew.

Polish is a difficult language with a rich and ancient literature. Besides the spelling looking like it was taken off an eye chart, the grammar is complex and well defined. The Poles love their language, love to hear other people try to use it, and readily correct mistakes. A Polish friend of mine in high school used to counter the ubiquitous Polack jokes with the retort, "Do you speak Polish?" When the negative answer came back, he shut the heckler up with, "How does it feel to be dumber than a Polack?"

"Wo gehen Sie?" asked the guard in simple German, assuming we understood that language.

"Wroclaw," answered Greg, pronouncing it "rot-slaw."

full of cheer and bonhomie. It was in the parking lot that our meal was soured by the first exhibition I would see of that omnipresent blight on Polish society, alcoholism.

Four well inebriated young men were having a serious discussion which led up to one of them punching another full in the face. There was a resounding crack. The man struck just stood there, swaying as if uncertain as to whether he should fall down or punch back. His friend punched him again from that flat-footed stance so characteristic of the Eastern European and Russian Olympic boxers and the swaying man fell straight over backwards landing flat on his back in a puddle. He lay there for a while until his other friends helped him up. They held a rag to his nose, which was bleeding and probably broken. Then all three put their arms around his shoulders and under his armpits and in a sloppy, drunken stagger headed for home, an eight-legged raft of wet, blabbering, wretched and barely sentient humanity.

The next day was spent at a leisurely pace cleaning things up, drying things out (when it wasn't raining) and pretty much relaxing. That afternoon when it began to get dark we had plans for some kind of secret rendezvous.

I knew nothing at all of the details. Only Dave and Greg would go to meet somebody and discuss something. My job was to drive them there and back. I didn't need to know any more than that.

We examined our route on the map before we left leaving no markings on it to indicate our true destination. Then we left with me driving. I took the two of them to an easy to find street, presumably within comfortable walking distance of the contact's house and dropped them off. My instructions were to go park somewhere out of sight and come back in two hours. I was to drive up that street every half hour from that time on until they reappeared. If they weren't back by midnight, I'd return to the campground and wait for them there.

After dropping them off, I decided to take the van out of town a few kilometers and park on some side street out of sight. The problem with driving a Dutch VW van in an Eastern Bloc country is that it attracts attention. Parked on an open street, it might attract curious citizens interested in making conversation. Or a transaction. Trade in black market dollars was brisk and tourists were often hit up to exchange money at very lucrative rates. Looking back over the years, I have to say that in my experience, the Poles out-shined all the others at doing business under the table. Indeed, the small legal flea market in Hungary is still called the Polish Market.

I headed out of town on the same street from which I would, hopefully, pick up Greg and Dave in two hours time. A few meters beyond a railroad crossing I found a muddy side road which fit my purposes perfectly. There was a stand of trees and a lot of brush along the side into which I pulled the car and parked. I turned off the motor, dowsed the lights and enjoyed the silence.

Traffic was indeed rare. In fact, over the next hour the only thing I saw on the main road was a horse-drawn carriage loaded with some kind of farm produce, maybe sugar beets. Impossible to tell in the darkness.

The night was completely overcast and it sprinkled from time to time, just as it had almost every day for as long as we had been on the road.

"Some August!" I thought to myself.

Then I heard the sound of a truck. No, trucks. Big trucks. But I couldn't see any lights in the darkness.

"Strange," I thought.

Then a blacked out military vehicle pulled up just past the crossroads less than a hundred yards from where I was hiding. Out jumped a squad of policemen or maybe soldiers in full equipment and carrying Kalashnikovs. The fellow in charge started giving orders.

My heart leapt into my throat.

What to do? I reached for the ignition key torn between starting up and making a run for it and sitting there and letting them find me. Then I thought that I might have a better chance in the dark night on foot. My pulse pounded loudly in my ears.

Then I got a grip on myself. The armed, uniformed men had fanned out to cover the railway crossing, but weren't doing anything else. It was a security detail for some convoy soon to follow. As it got quieter, the sound of the trucks got louder.

Then they appeared in the gloom, blacked out and crawling at a snail's pace along the road. They were big tractor-trailer rigs, eighteen in all, transporting something huge.

"Maybe missiles," I said to myself. That would explain the blackout.

"No, it wouldn't be missiles. If it were missiles there would be a lot more security involved."

"Yeah, but security itself attracts attention. Maybe this way was better for secrecy."

I argued with myself back and forth as I counted the huge transports, marveling at my luck at seeing something this important by accident. I decided to drive by the US embassy and file a spot report on our way home. Sure, it may be only an insignificant bit of construction material being hauled to build some general a dacha, but who knows? A cardinal rule in intelligence gathering is to never turn down any information no matter how seemingly insignificant.

It was all over in fifteen minutes. I noted the time and knew I could remember the location on a map. Then I waited out the rest of the agreed two hours and headed back to pick up the guys.

They were right where they said they'd be as I drove along and opened the doors. They jumped in without a word and we headed off toward the campground.

"How did it go?" I asked.

"Just fine. No problems at all," Dave answered.

I let the silence hang in the air for a minute and realized I wasn't going to get anything else out of either of them. I didn't mention the trucks either. Then Greg started telling us about the Baptist church we were going to visit in two days. It would be unforgettable, he promised.

On Sunday morning we arose with the dawn. At least it was time for dawn. With the clouds and the rain, I didn't see much in the way of proof.

We cleaned ourselves up as much as we could with cold water from the latrine, put on our nicest wrinkled camping clothes, broke camp and moved out in the direction of the quaintest little Polish village you could imagine, complete with a crystal clear mountain stream, nestled among the forested mountains.

So far we had seen very little of the East besides the dirty cities, the primitive campgrounds and boring flat countryside. But this was different. Everything was so fresh and clean, even the rain seemed nice. In fact, it was quite a lot like Washington State where I grew up except somebody had run the clock back fifty years.

The houses were simple and old, but clean and neat, except where chicken coops and pig pens were found. The people were different, too. They seemed happier. Their step was lighter. They stared at our van just like the city people did, but when they stared, they smiled and waved.

We pulled up to a pretty little country church situated in a small green meadow on the edge of the little town. It was already packed and people were standing outside the open windows in the rain and listening to the sermon. Now and again the congregation would burst into song, unaccompanied by piano or organ, unled by song leader and unaided by hymnals. The chorus drifted through the air across the town and people lifted their heads attentively, as though sniffing the breeze for the aroma of something good coming out of the oven.

Poland is almost all Catholic, but this was a Baptist congregation. I detected no hint of animosity the whole time I was there of either denomination for the other. I would find as the months passed that there was a remarkable amount of cooperation between denominations, Catholics helping Protestants and vice versa. Only a fool fights in a burning house, as they say.

It rained. Those who had umbrellas shared them. Those who did not used old newspaper. I stood outside the window for over an hour, as interested in the crowd around me as I was in the meeting. The service went on and on, rotating from one short sermon, to a song, to a prayer in which everybody seemed to participate together. The effect of everybody praying at once was rather like being inside a bee hive. The din rose and fell with the emotion of the leader and after some minutes, when the tone felt just right, a loud "amen" was sounded and echoed by the congregation. Then another song, another sermon, and so on.

I wasn't the least bit tired after almost two hours of this and had completely forgotten about the others. Then I heard some words from inside that sounded very much like an introduction (I couldn't see a thing). Words sounding like "americanski" and "hollandia" caught my attention and then I became aware of the sea of friendly faces smiling and nodding at me and probably at the others as well, wherever they were. No way could we have just blended into this crowd.

Then Greg, in a pressed and immaculate suit and tie appeared at the back door, was ushered up to the front and gave greetings from the believers in Holland and America. I have no idea how he managed to even keep a suit in that condition, let alone find someplace to change after we had arrived. But he did and he strode to the podium looking like he had never set foot inside a campground in his life. What was more, it was obvious that he had been in this town before. People seemed to recognize him and considered him something of a celebrity. I was amazed.

It wasn't long after Greg spoke that the meeting ended. But nobody went home. Band instruments began to appear, complete with a tuba. The crowd started to congeal into a line of sorts. I had no idea what was going on, but it looked like there was going to be a parade of some kind.

And a parade it was. We marched right through the center of town, singing and playing hymns, down to the river's edge. A public baptism followed, the pastor dipping the white-robed converts swiftly under surface and the deacons helping them in and out of the cold water. There were old and young being baptized, the ritual initiated by the pastor calling for their public confession of faith as he held the candidate's hand and shoulder, followed by the affirmation, the immersion and finished by the verse of a hymn sung by all. The only break in the process occurred when a string of three teenage girls, with the usual European contempt for women's foundation garments, got baptized and came up in wet clinging linen, which hid nothing of their blooming femininity. The first one got all the way through the crowd to her mother before someone could wrap a blanket around her. The second teenager made it only to the river bank and the third had Mom with a blanket waiting for her at the pastor's side.

"Yep, they're Baptists, alright," cracked Dave out of the side of his mouth.

Then we all lined up again and marched back through town back to the church.

"What's all this I hear about religious persecution in these parts?" I thought to myself.

After the crowd began to break up, Greg got us all invited to stay the night in a Polish family's house. Dave explained that it was technically against the rules, but this was an exception. We were in no danger from the authorities and it would be bad form to turn down their hospitality.

We parked the car in the fenced-in yard of a member of the church, took our bags (each of us carried a little overnight case, Greg had a suitcase and his medicine bag) and walked out of town in the company of those we would be staying with. They insisted on carrying our luggage for us and we chatted pleasantly throughout the hike. Again, as in Germany, with bits and pieces of languages we knew, we conversed without any serious barrier.

After about half a mile we came to a path leading up into the woods from the main road. It had stopped raining, but it was still wet and the path was a bit treacherous. Even in good weather no car could have negotiated it. The Poles said they had a horse that could make it but they only used him to haul things.

When we reached the top of the path the forest opened onto a beautiful house of rough hewn wood, almost like a log cabin. There was smoke coming from the chimney and beyond the house I could see a barn, the outhouse, and a field dotted by haystacks. To the right downhill from the house ran a little brook.

Foreigners, even relatives, could not stay in the Romanian citizens' home legally and all contact with foreigners had to be reported to the police. Even to answer a tourist's request for directions risked being picked up and questioned by the police, who often used some pretty rough techniques to get answers.

When it got dark, they lit the kerosene lamps and I started to feel a little hungry again. After tea I had gone out for a little hike in the woods with the kids, who showed me everything they owned, where they played, how they fetched water from the stream, and whose chicken was whose. It had been a pleasant afternoon, and now it was bath time for the kids.

As the kids ate their supper of sliced sausages, butter, jam and bread, Grandma got the big wash tub down from the wall, put it on the floor by the furnace, mixed the hot and cold water to just the right temperature and then scrubbed down each little one from head to toe, rubbed them dry and put them into their clean pajamas. They waved goodnight to us as Grandma packed them off to tell them their bedtime story.

Then we all ate a similar supper and sat down to more tea and juice. Soon afterwards, Greg started to look sleepy, so our hosts showed him which bed was his, and with very little encouragement, he started to get ready to turn in. Dave, Ruth, Susan and I were still in a sociable mood, so we stayed up to talk with our hosts. Anyway, we knew Greg would be about a half an hour before he would be ready to hit the hay, so we delayed bedtime for a while. I am still not sure how they did it, but our hosts had arranged it so that we each had a bed.

When we finally decided to turn in, I went into the room Dave and I would be sharing with Greg. It was much too warm, so I asked Dave if he'd mind if I opened the window a crack. He said, "By all means," so I did and got ready for bed. Then Greg, who we both thought was asleep, got up, closed the window firmly, got back into bed with the comment, "You both know I catch cold if I sleep with the window open." Dave and I just looked at each other, shrugged, and got into bed. Sometimes Greg's hypochondria could get a little annoying. It was also a sign that the trip was coming to an end and we were beginning to get on each other's nerves.

The next day we moved on and found a campsite outside Lodz (pronounced 'Wootch'), set up camp and prepared for our last foray in enemy territory. Greg and I would attempt to make contact with a believer our people had worked with before while the rest stayed back at camp.

Again it was drizzling as we set off for a town that Greg was familiar with. I drove while he navigated, rarely needing to consult the map.

"Do we need gas?" he asked.

"Nope. The gauge says half full," I answered.

"We'll tank up on the way back," he said.

As we were driving through the little town I pulled over and we consulted the map together. Greg explained to me just where the contact's house was in relation to where we were. We said a short prayer for safety and I turned the key to restart the engine. The motor choked and spluttered a bit, then roared to life only to cough and stall. Repeated attempts to get it to run were only met with failure.

"What's wrong?" asked Greg.

"Don't know. Sounds like we're out of gas. Or maybe there's water in the fuel line. I'd better check under the hood," I said and with that got out in the rain to have a look. A quick survey of the engine showed no obvious cause for the problem. I scraped the distributor, cleaned and reseated the spark plug connections, peeked into the carburetor, but found nothing out of the ordinary. We needed a mechanic.

"We can't do that!" said Greg. "Nobody must find out we're here!"

"So what do you suggest? I can't think of anything else to do."

After a pause he acquiesced. "Okay. You go find a private mechanic and I'll stay here with the car." But first, we prayed.

"Oh God, we don't know why…"

With my Berlitz Polish phrase book firmly in hand, I set out to find a person who could repair our vehicle. It turned out to be surprisingly easy. By asking "Where is the nearest mechanic?" in Polish and pointing to the phrase in the book, people on the street very politely directed me to the home of a German-Pole who had a garage. Not only was it great for me that I'd be able to talk to him in a language I understood, he was closed for the day and that meant he had no other business. If I offered him enough money, he would certainly help us.

As I walked up to the door, I met his elderly wife coming out. I asked her whether the mechanic was home and she said that her husband was indeed in. Then she scurried off to do some shopping.

I was met at the door by a straight-backed, fit working man of retirement age but who didn't look a day over fifty. Briefly I explained our problem to him and that we would gladly pay extra for the help we so badly needed. He considered the situation for minute and said yes, he would be glad to help.

We hopped into his car and drove back to the van where by this time, Greg was in a stew. "Thank God, uh, Goodness your back! Have him fix the car and we'll be off."

The mechanic tried the key with the same results I had. Then he got out, looked under the hood, took a wrench out of his pocket, loosened the fuel line and let a little dribble out while he watched. "Water in the fuel line," he said with finality.

"Ask him what we need to do," Greg directed. I asked and translated back his answer, which was that we had to drain the line, the gas tank and fill it up with gas again.

"You have spare gas in the can, don't you?" the mechanic asked, having noted the red container on the ground next to the door. Greg had taken it out.

"Of course," I said automatically.

"No we don't," Greg countered.

"Why? I mean, what happened to our gas?" I asked.

"I, uh, poured it out as a gesture of faith believing God would heal the engine," Greg admitted.

"Oh," I said, biting off an unkind comment.

BULGARIA

My first step while resting up from the trip to the DDR and Poland was to find out as much as I could about the tactics and relative success of the literature smuggling operations. The mission had suffered several setbacks in the few years prior to my joining in 1977. Our people were being picked up at the borders with greater frequency. Literature and vehicles were confiscated and the couriers fined and held for questioning. Under interrogation our people were divulging to the Communists very damaging information about unregistered churches. What was worse, often after being interrogated and released, the missionary sometimes wrote a book about the experience, revealing important information to any Eastern European intelligence service that might take the time to read it. There were a lot of copy-cat books being printed modeled after Brother Andrew's "God's Smuggler."

Often the border police would let the smugglers through and follow them to the contacts' houses, so operations were getting ever more complicated and expensive to counter this tactic. The information gathering and processing system of the mission was badly in need of organization. There

I took the train up to Ermelo and called for someone to pick me up. I was brought to the Garage, or so it was called, by the operations officer, Henk, the brother of Paul. After a few introductions, Henk showed me the van we would be taking with its clever secret compartment under the floor.

It would be a determined guard indeed who could find it. The compartment was only partly filled with literature, but we would pick up just over a hundred Bulgarian Bibles at the Licht im Osten (Light in the East), a German mission in Stuttgart on our way. I would be leaving off the books, mostly by authors like Billy Graham, David Wilkerson and Corrie ten Boom at a separate contact from where I would leave the Bibles. Henk showed me how to pack them so that there would be no hollow sound if the guards started tapping around.

After that, Henk took me into his private office and briefed me on my assignment. With a map of Bulgaria in front of us, he showed me the borders he wanted me to use and said to keep a sharp eye out for the thoroughness of the searches, not only of our car, but of the others as well. We should go in through Yugoslavia and out through Greece. He gave me folders on each of our contacts including background information and maps, both marked and unmarked. He told me to memorize everything carefully, since, except for the unmarked maps, I could take no written information in with me. I could take some Xerox copies of important details with me as far as the Yugoslavian border if I wanted, but I must be sure to destroy them all before we went in. Since some of the contacts had not been seen in years, I should do my best to remember details to update the mission's files when I got back. And to try to bring out some up-to-date maps.

He left me alone for a half an hour to study my assignment. I made a few copies of the more important things, put them together with the unmarked maps and then we went to his house to have lunch with his family.

From there, Henk called his friend who went by the pseudonym of Brother Piet. Virtually all of us used pseudonyms both in our travels into the East and on deputation work in the West. Brother Piet was one of legends in the mission on par with Brother Andrew (also a pseudonym, by the way). An elderly biologist with a heart condition, he had done quite a lot of work in Romania and Bulgaria, two of the worst places in those days. When I met him, he was semi-retired and rarely traveled any more due to his heart. Our meeting left an indelible impression on me.

Henk drove me to Piet's house after lunch and left me there, saying he would be back for me in an hour. I walked to the door and pushed the bell button.

The figure that greeted me was a tall, thin, elderly Dutchman who spoke perfect English and, although he smiled not at all, had a kindly air about him. He beckoned me inside.

His house had the feel of the presence of a Dutch housewife, so neat and so clean. But the fact that he seated me in his study and prepared the tea himself left me to wonder whether he might be a widower. I didn't know much about the personal side of Piet at all.

Waiving the unnecessary "how do you like Holland?" kind of pleasantries, he got right down to business.

"When do you plan to leave for Bulgaria?" he asked.

"Tomorrow," I said.

"Will you be picking up the large-print Bulgarian Bibles in Stuttgart?" he asked.

"Yes."

"Good. They are a special request from a special person. While in Stuttgart, be sure to say nothing of the details of your trip to anyone there. They are good people, but they don't need to know anything about your trip, and certainly not in advance. I can't emphasize enough that you must be cautious."

I was going to point out that my military training taught me the basics of operational security and that I understood about caution, but thought that it would be wiser just to keep quiet and listen. Not to mention polite.

He continued on with general advice about what to do and not to do. Make sure I'm not followed to the Christians' houses. Never let anyone outside of the team in the car. Don't take out any letters or messages when we leave Bulgaria.

"The Bulgarians are a people very different from any other in Europe," he said. "They are a people given to intrigue and treachery. Their history has bred into them a tradition of spying on and betraying each other, even family members."

I knew something of that. Bulgaria has spent some five hundred years under Turkish rule and been on the losing side of almost every war it ever fought. Even their language has a rare and unusual point of grammar called the "hearsay tense." From the conjugation of the verb one can tell whether the information reported is believed to be fact or just rumor.

"In politics they are more Catholic than the Pope, which is to say, more Stalinist than the Russians, even the Romanians. The KGB uses Bulgarian assassins to do jobs they won't touch. Nothing is too dirty for them and they are involved in everything from training terrorists to distributing heroin. Be very, very careful," he emphasized again.

Then, "How is your Bulgarian?"

"I graduated top in my class. It should be pretty good," I answered. I had spent all of 1974 at the Defense Language Institute in Monterey learning the language as a soldier.

"Have you ever spent time among Bulgarians or been to Bulgaria before?"

"No," I admitted. All of my teachers were over sixty and sitting in a classroom isn't quite the same as spending time in society.

"Then it would be safe to say that you will be easily spotted for a foreigner," he concluded. That hurt, but I don't know why. It was nothing to be ashamed of and it was true. I should have recognized that little bruise to my ego as a signal that I had a higher opinion of myself than I should have had. "A man has got to know his limitations," as Dirty Harry aptly put it.

"But you can understand the spoken language well enough," he said, more as a question.

"Sure," I said. Of that, I was certain regardless of how old my teachers had been. I had listened to hundreds of hours of Bulgarian radio tapes while in language school.

"Good. I am particularly interested in you getting some information from two people. The first is a policeman who had allegedly converted, but his story sounds a little fishy to me. I want you to meet him and hear his whole story. Bear in mind that he may be a double agent or perhaps even psychotic. I won't tell you any details so you can keep an open mind. But we must talk about him when you get back. You can ask around at the Baptist church you will visit in Sofia.

The second person you must meet is old Pastor Simon in Shumen. He is the one you will be giving the large-print Bibles to. He is very wise and knows more about the Underground Church in Bulgaria than any man alive. He is close to ninety now and has spent over thirteen years in prison. But his mind is sharp. He may have some new people for you to meet to expand our contacts. Tell him you were sent by me and ask about the rain. He will confide in you."

"The rain?" I asked.

"That is our little private code. When you return, tell me what he told you about the rain."

About then Henk showed up at the door and Piet let him in. After a little friendly conversation, Piet turned me over to Henk with an avuncular pat on the shoulder and one last admonition to be very, very careful. I left filled with the mixed feelings of anticipation and trepidation.

In driving the van out of the Garage, it struck me just how easy it would be for the Communists to shut the place down if they wanted to. There must be hundreds of people who know what goes on there and with an organization whose annual budget exceeds a million dollars, it would be easy indeed to find the address from any of their PR material. All one would have to do would be to have somebody watch the front gate and take down the license numbers of all the vehicles that came and left. Any vehicle with one of those license numbers that appeared on any border would get detained and searched. That uneasy thought accompanied me all the way back to the Farm.

The next day we left for Bulgaria. The whole drive was uneventful, even pleasant with four people to share the wheel. We got the Bibles in Stuttgart – which I stored away by myself – and overnighted there. The next day we made Vienna, or more specifically, House Edelweiss.

House Edelweiss is the base of the Toronto Christian Mission in Austria. It is a big Bavarian lodge nestled in the Vienna Woods and incomparably nicer than the farm we lived at in Holland. I found myself wishing that I had run into TCM before I met Paul. The air was fresh, the woods were peaceful, and there was even a swimming pool. The lodge itself had a history going back over a hundred years involving the murder of some member of the Hapsburg family on the premises. And for people like Susan and myself who really wanted to practice our German, it was ideal. Many of the staff didn't even speak English. It also made more sense to have a mission within an hour of the borders of Czechoslovakia, Hungary and Yugoslavia than as far away as Holland.

They welcomed us, fed us, let us rest up and take a swim. Unfortunately for Tracy, she didn't have a one-piece suit with her and the rules didn't allow for even boys and

I briefly consulted my map with a little penlight shaded by red cellophane and decided to try the next street over. The bags were heavy and my arms already ached. I had three of the bags, but I knew Tracy must be hurting, too. We found a place under a tree where there was some trash, left the bags there and moved off to the other side of the road.

"I'm going to scout up ahead before we carry these things all the way. You wait here out of sight and keep an eye open. I'll be back in a few minutes," I whispered.

Just then we heard a car approaching and saw the headlights before it turned the corner and headed toward us.

"Put your arms around me, quick!" I hissed. We stood there in the shadows, looking (I hoped) like two lovers on a clandestine rendezvous. Our hearts were certainly doing a good imitation. Tracy was trembling. Maybe I was, too.

When the car was gone, I struck out for the target house. Moving swiftly through the shadows, I found it with no trouble. The intersection was a little too well lit for my tastes, so I waited in the dark until I was sure that the only sound I wasn't imagining was my own heart pounding in my ears. Then I walked quickly to the gate, opened it (it creaked), found the door to the cellar and tried it. It was unlocked. Good.

When I got back to Tracy, I asked her whether she had seen anybody.

"I saw two people up the road going the other direction about five minutes ago," she said.

"Do you think they're gone?" I asked.

"Yeah."

"Shall we go for it?"

"Okay."

We picked up the bags and started off down the dark street, keeping as best we could to the shadows. It was now close to 11:00.

Things were going fine when all of a sudden, out of a side alley stepped two big men. They were so close to us that even in the dark I could read the writing on their red arm bands. They were members of the Citizens' Militia, a civilian organization that acts as an auxiliary to the police. They patrol the streets after dark and are alleged to take their job very seriously.

I cannot imagine anything more suspicious than two Americans carrying five large bags of Bibles down the back streets of Sofia, Bulgaria, after curfew. Yet they didn't stop us, didn't look at us, didn't even break stride. It was as though God had suddenly made Tracy and me invisible. We kept right on walking.

When we arrived at the house, we paused to check out the area and, seeing and hearing nothing, walked to the gate, opened it (this time it didn't creak), opened the cellar door and descended the stairs. At the bottom stair, I kicked over an empty milk bucket with a crash.

When our hearts started beating again, we dropped the bags of Bibles on the floor and scrambled out of there as fast as we could. Then we made our way back to the pick up point by a different route.

By the time we got there, the excitement and adrenaline surge had worn off leaving a pleasant afterglow. Although we were far from out of danger, the worst was over. We waited for Don to show up.

And waited and waited.

After an hour, we were forced to accept that Don was not coming back for us and we had a 14 kilometer hike ahead of us in the cool Bulgarian night.

It could have been a pleasant stroll, but we were tired and hungry. Moreover, I was a little worried about what Don might do. What if he left for the border before we reached the campground?

Another annoyance was the consequence of the Bulgarian economy still making abundant use of ox and horse carts. The roads were strewn with manure which we, in the dim light, had trouble avoiding.

Then, a car loaded with three drunken musicians pulled up and offered us a ride.

"Gde otivate?" (Where are you going?)

"V Kemping." (To the campground.)

"Hn, taka. Chuzhdentsi. Ot gde?" (Oh, you're foreign. Where are you from?)

"Amerika."

"Ah! Amerika! Elvis Presley! Kom on averybady! Ladt da good times roll!"

It was a fun, if somewhat scary, ride. They couldn't speak English, but they knew all the words to all the popular songs. They let us off at the gate, refused the money I offered, and drove off.

Getting into the campground at 2:00 a.m. wasn't that easy either since we didn't have our passports on us, but after a lecture from the night watchman about curfew, he finally let us in.

When I plopped into our tent, Don woke up.

"What happened to you? Get lost?" I asked.

"No. I did just like you said. Drove up that street every fifteen minutes for two hours and then came on back here."

"We were back before two hours, but didn't see you. Are you sure you were on the right street?"

"Pretty sure. But, to tell the truth, the markings weren't all that clear. Sorry if I let you down," he apologized.

"No, you did just fine. Anyway, we're back and everything came off without a hitch," I said.

Don wanted to hear the whole story but I was so tired I said we'd tell both of them all about it in the morning. I think I was asleep before my head hit the air mattress.

The next day we left for Shumen. I was particularly looking forward to meeting Pastor Simon. The campground we found that afternoon was little more than a side road into somebody's plum orchard. Except for a water spigot, there were no facilities, but neither were there many people. As far as the four of us were concerned, it was just fine.

We drove into town and found Simon's place without any trouble. He was home with his eighty-something-year-old wife. They lived in a pleasant, simple little cottage surrounded by a garden filled with fruits and vegetables. Grape vines covered the walls. They were just getting ready to have a little afternoon refreshment on a hot August day when we arrived.

Simon looked all the world like George Burns to me, complete with thick glasses. Only the cigar was missing.

of course because of the language, so for the rest of the crew, it was time to look like real vacationers.

We set up camp and, after refusing a few Polish campers who wanted to change money, headed for the beach.

The beach was beautiful from afar, but when you started walking on it, you suddenly encountered the old manure problem again. Only on the beach, it wasn't horse or cow manure. There were no toilets or wash facilities near the beach, so apparently the custom is to just relieve oneself right on the beach while covered with a towel.

Tracy and I got to the water and simultaneously made a dive into the waves. That action was abruptly halted by a whistle and a shout from one of the life guards. "No swimming! Only up to the knees!" and he pointed to a sign explaining that wading only was allowed. We were crushed but in no position to argue. He was the first lifeguard I had ever seen in my life with a pistol. There was even a life guard tower with a gun port in it not far away. We settled for a stroll down the beach instead, joking about whether any of our friends would believe we had been thrown out of the Black sea by a gun-toting lifeguard.

"Stop drowning or I'll shoot!"

That afternoon, I took a little walk through town and looked up Simon's Baptist colleague. He was, just as Simon described, a very cautious man, but with a very friendly wife. We talked a little and I asked where I might buy a Bulgarian-English dictionary in town. She immediately brought out one and gave it to me. I tried to refuse, but she insisted. Besides, for all their faults, the Communists had made all printed matter in their world very cheap. Before I left, we had prayer together and the lady wrapped up a nice little vase for me to "take home to my mother."

The next day, we decided to drive hard to Sofia. I only wanted to meet this converted policeman Piet had told me about before we left the country. We stayed at the same campground as before and I went into town alone to meet my first contacts. They would know where to find the policeman and advise me on his reliability. Also, I was curious about the incident with the police car that night and how the literature we had dropped off had been received.

When I showed up at their door, they welcomed me like family. No, nothing had happened after I left that night and the "bread" was already being distributed. With the television turned up, I asked them about this policeman. Did they know him, and was he reliable?

"Oh, yes! Absolutely reliable."

"Could I possibly meet him?" I asked.

"Of course. You already know the way to his house. It was his cellar in which you left the books." They would arrange for me to meet him the following morning.

Back at camp, I told the others that the following day, if all went well, we would leave Bulgaria. We would break camp early and I planned to have a talk with the policeman in the morning while they waited in the parked car. From there we would head south and be in Greece that afternoon. There were cheers all around.

The next morning, after my usual cold shower and encounter with the cleaning lady, we packed up. Inspired by Susan's generosity, I snatched a couple of jars of Nescafe into a campground late that afternoon, Tracy was already chafing at the bit to get down to the water. God help the person who stood between her and finally getting a swim! And after the long, hot ride, I was almost as eager as she.

The sun was just about to set as we got the tents up. Don and Susan volunteered to cook supper while Tracy and I reconnoitered the beach.

The shore by the campground turned out not to be a beach at all but just a place where the rocks met the ocean. The beach was up the road a ways, so on we walked. When we came to the actual beach, there was a turnstile and a booth to pay an entrance fee. We didn't mind the small cost at all, but the beach closed for the evening and, while we could leave whenever we wanted, if we wanted in, it would have to be now before the sun went down.

We hadn't brought our swim suits or towels, as we intended only to scout the place out and return later for a leisurely swim after dinner. Now it looked like even that might not be possible. As we strolled along the pebbly beach, Tracy muttered under her breath that she was getting a swim tonight by hook or crook and I sympathized. The beauty of the Adriatic lapping gently against the shore backlit by the fading orange and red of the sunset only served to steel our resolve.

The solution to our problem came completely unexpectedly. In our haste, we hadn't read the sign as we entered the gate. But the few bathers that remained on the beach demonstrated that we had missed something important.

We were on a nudist beach.

"Trace, this is too perfect," I said. "I'm going for a swim, if you don't mind looking the other way until I get into the water."

"I'm coming in, too," she said firmly, and then chuckled, "But I don't think we should tell Don and Susan."

"Or write it up in our mission report," I added with a smile, already pulling off my shirt.

I got into the water and turned around to tell Tracy that she could start if she wanted, but she was already out of her clothes and picking her way gingerly through the rough pebbles. I turned away quickly. She splashed into the water and broke into a vigorous breast stroke, then rolled over about twenty yards away and floated on her back mumbling, "There is a God, there is a God..." in ecstasy.

It got dark and we stayed in the sea paddling around, talking, or just floating in our own thoughts giving no concern for the time. I reflected on all we had been through, what we had risked for the cause of Christ, what we had accomplished, and what I had learned. I thought of how silly and superficial all the program-oriented game playing that made up so much of my Christianity until then now seemed. How tragic it would have been never to have found these people, these magnificent believers, for whom their faith was a paradoxical choice between life and death! Choose death and live.

"A wet man does not fear the rain." Such wisdom!

The symbology of Tracy and me floating naked in the sea seemed appropriate. It was for both of us a holy moment, like the creation of new life, a moment of birth following a long mundane gestation in America with a difficult labor in Bulgaria.

We came out of the water feeling pure, cleansed and refreshed. The darkness hid our nakedness and we lay a polite distance from each other on the warm rocks talking as we dried in the cool air of evening. We felt neither shame nor lust, and strangest of all, it all seemed fitting and as things should be, as though Christians walked around outside naked together all the time. Heaven should feel like that.

Getting back into our clothes felt positively obscene.

When we got back to Don and Susan, supper was cold and they both gave us that knowing look. Just as well, I thought, if they think we have a romance going. We couldn't tell anybody what we had really done, anyway.

GOING FULL TIME

"I know! Faith And Realistic Teaching – FART!" suggested Lanny.

"Or how about Basic Universal Lines and Limits of Spiritual Healing In Theology," added Dave.

"Or Christian Religious Activity Principles," said Mary.

Lanson Ross, along with his wife Mary and two sons Lanny and Dave were having a field day helping – or rather, not helping – Lanson and me come up with a good name for my project. Lanson knew a lot about raising money for mission projects, so I sought him out at earliest opportunity for advice when I got back to the States.

We brainstormed fruitlessly around their kitchen table for the better part of half an hour to come up with a name that succinctly stated what I wanted to do: put together a basic pastor's study library for Eastern European ministers. We eventually settled on Effort for the Advance of Scriptural Teaching – EAST – but not before Lanny, Dave and Mary came up with a couple dozen better, if unusable, acronyms. Lanson and Mary helped me set up the non-profit corporation and get started with fund raising. They thought the idea would be well received, but I would have to down play the choice of systematic theology. You'll never get a large number of Christians to agree on the best Bible teaching available, so it's better not to make a big deal out of it.

But it is a big deal. There was a lot of nonsense being spread around in the unregistered churches and that was precisely what I wanted to counter. I started looking around for something systematic and solid, simple enough for the layman but complete enough for a pastor. I came upon a series that seemed for meet the need both for young pastors and for me.

"The Word of God is alive and powerful, sharper than any two-edged sword, piercing even to the dividing asunder ..."

I listened to the first cassette tape in a series of Basic Bible Doctrine by Lieutenant Colonel (Retired) Robert B. Thieme, Jr., pastor of Berachah Church in Houston, Texas, a man whose teaching and example would profoundly influence my life. I knew that I wanted nothing more badly in life than to work with the Underground Church in Eastern Europe. All the other important things in my life would be given second place. Such a noble call demanded my undivided devotion. Not even marriage or a secular profession could be allowed to stand in my way. Although I felt uniquely prepared for this calling I still needed some work in systematic theology.

My brother Glenn, then a student at Dallas Theological Seminary, made some recommendations for home-study courses prepared by qualified Bible teachers, mostly on cassette tape. I was looking for something systematic, designed to take a lay person from the basics up through a comprehensive survey of Christian theology, sort of a mini-seminary course.

There were several promising courses among those recommended to me, but Thieme's teaching would eventually win out over the rest. His methodology was simple; he called it ICE teaching. ICE stands for Isogogics (putting the Bible into the culture and times in which it was written), Categories (comparing scripture with scripture to develop the doctrines by category), and Exegesis (translation and interpretation from the original languages). The ICE system provided a methodology for me to examine and interpret the scriptures which developed in me a badly needed confidence regarding the Word. ICE teaching was to theology what the scientific method was to research, the engine of knowledge.

Thieme had his detractors. People either loved him or hated him. For me, personality conflicts were entirely immaterial. I was after solid teaching and the personality or style of the teacher made no difference. I nevertheless made a careful effort to research his theology involving interviews with several Bible scholars and a trip to his church in Houston and to Dallas Theological Seminary, his alma mater, to gather every criticism I could find in print. I found all objections raised against this man to be minor at best, usually *ad hominem*, and his positive contributions to theology to be substantial. It was his methodology that stood out more than anything else. With the ICE method, a student would not follow long on a path of false teaching without seeing the error.

In 1977, Bob Thieme was just what I needed.

where Paul was and how I was to get started on the Bulgaria project. While waiting I took the time to get acquainted with the staff at the Farm.

The permanent staff was a microcosm of five people who embodied as wide a range of Christian vice and virtue as had ever been assembled in one place on the planet. When you combined them with the semi-permanent staff and the summer missionaries from all walks of Christendom, you have real world sitcom. A healthy sense of humor was probably the most useful survival tool a person could possess.

Jan Vanderwald, the local chief of staff, was the pastor of a local church on Sundays. Although a competent administrator, he was treacherously two-faced. He maintained a facade of a sweetness and love which veiled but didn't hide his favorite hobby of sewing discord among brethren at every opportunity. He could look a person in the eye, tell him how great it was to have him at the mission, and the minute that person left the room tell somebody else what a big mistake it was to invite him. He never said an unkind word to me or criticized me in any way all the months I was there, though his parting comment would be that he knew all along that I wouldn't work out and was against it from the start.

Joop Pieterzoon was a high-strung red-haired and balding Dutchman who had an incisive and logical mind that I admired. Because of his nervous nature, he had no business doing field work, but Paul had put him exactly where he belonged. He was our intelligence officer tasked with sorting out all the information the mission dealt with, classifying it and seeing that the appropriate people got it. I would work closely with Joop over my stint at the mission and come to appreciate him more and more the better I got to know him. It was a sad day when he eventually moved on to another mission, unable to cope with the vacillations of our leader.

Melissa, or Millie as she liked to be called, our secretary and receptionist was Paul's American wife. She was a pleasant and intelligent girl whose company I always enjoyed. She could be straight forward when problems arose but was never offensive. She was, in short, the perfect executive secretary and made up for a lot of her husband's shortcomings.

Jack and his wife Mary were in charge of running the Farm. They oversaw the reconstruction, fed and housed everybody and generally organized things. Jack is the only former monk I have ever met. His most prominent personality trait was his asceticism, which he carried out to an artistic degree. Due to his regular fasting and praying, he was an emaciated man, prone to common ailments such as colds and flu. Nevertheless, you had to look hard to find out when he was engaging in his personal chastisement of the body, as he never let on when he was fasting or what he was giving up. Like Jan, he had an attraction to the sins and peccadilloes of others, but unlike Jan, he approached them with an attitude of healing rather than exacerbation.

There was an American summer missionary that year, Bob, a lovable and talkative fellow who was well liked by most of us. He was rotund, jocular and reminded me a lot of the comedian John Candy. One afternoon Mary, who oversaw the kitchen, brought out a plate of cookies for us to enjoy while we worked and said for us to help ourselves. Bob enthusiastically took a handful, put one in his mouth and the rest in his pocket and went back to work.

Later that afternoon, while Bob and his wife were in town shopping, we had coffee and Jan started in.

"Did you see what Bob did? My goodness, I've never seen anything like it. He just took a bunch of cookies as if nobody else mattered," he said to Jack. I don't think Jack, or any of the rest of us had considered the event a big deal, but Jan thought it was outrageous. We had a prayer of blessing for the food, led by Jack as always, "Lord, we are grateful for your bounty and love. Thank you for this food set before us. And if Bob has a problem, we ask that you deal with it."

Jack saw the physical world as diametrically opposed to the spiritual world, and that viewpoint had some interesting consequences. It implied that natural feelings were generally wrong and, almost reflexively, Jack used to respond to things in exactly the opposite manner as one might expect. If you asked him whether he was hungry, tired or sick and he said no, then that meant he was hungry, tired or sick, but responding in the spiritually appropriate way. When he said he liked something, it meant he didn't like it, and if he said he loved you, watch out!

The single biggest social blunder I ever made at the mission was when I made a nude statue out of clay and named it after one of the girls on staff. I like to draw and for my birthday one of the girls, Helma, had given me a block of modeling clay. Over the months, I enjoyed hours of relaxation with that lump of clay, molding animals, faces and figures out of it over and over again. Once I managed to create a pretty nice torso and decided to show it to Helma.

Helma wasn't in the kitchen, where she usually worked, so I left it there with a note and a caricature of myself, done up as a Dutch Master, complete with beret, mallet and chisel, sitting in relaxed dignity before his recently completed masterpiece, which I entitled "Helmus."

That afternoon Jack came to see me for a visit.

"I really liked your statue," he said.

"Uh-oh," I thought to myself.

"It's just that Helma was rather embarrassed, so I had to get rid of it and assure her that you meant no harm by it," he went on.

"Is she there now?" I asked. "I'll go apologize immediately."

"No, she was pretty upset, so I sent her home," he concluded.

That left me feeling depressed the rest of the day. The rest of the staff carried on just as if nothing had happened, though. The next day at morning coffee time, I saw Helma and apologized.

"Helma, I'm sorry about the statue. I didn't mean to embarrass you," I said.

"It's okay. I doesn't matter," she said. She didn't seem to be embarrassed as much as I had been led to expect. As the luck of the duty roster would have it, I wound up in the kitchen after lunch washing dishes next to Helma and had a chance to talk with her a little more. She assured me that she had been flattered by the statue and was happy that I liked my present so much.

"Then why did you go home early yesterday? Jack said you were upset," I asked.

"No. I fasting. For God," she answered. "Jack throw away the 'Helmus' but I have the funny picture," she laughed.

I often wondered how Mary, who was voluptuously beautiful, managed to marry someone like Jack. True, Jack was an uncommonly virtuous man, easy to live with, honest and sincere. But such neurotic behavior must have taken its toll and I am sure that food wasn't the only physical pleasure that Jack commonly denied himself. Nevertheless, they managed to have a baby girl, Sylvia, who was the darling of the Farm.

After almost two weeks of his absence, I finally managed to collar Paul and attempt to clarify my status at the mission. Where was I to work? Where would I stay? What would be my duties? What about the Bulgaria project? He informed me, rather noncommittally, that I should just spend the summer like last summer, make a few trips as a courier and we'd talk about the Bulgaria project later.

"Later" never came.

However, I soon got assigned to a trip to Hungary which would have deep and permanent effects on the direction of my life.

HUNGARY

"The world's largest Egyptian museum is located here, in a little town in Eastern Hungary?" I asked.

"Yes, indeed, Brother Lloyd. Wait and you'll see," Greg assured me.

"Have you ever been inside?"

"No. Haven't had the time. It's huge. It would take two or three days to see it all."

My trip to Hungary with Greg and Carla in the summer of 1978 convinced me that Greg was completely off his rocker. It would be the last trip I would ever make with him. It was also on this trip that I first visited Debrecen, and the Free Church there, which would later become both my base of operations and my home. And not insignificantly, on this trip I would meet my future wife.

It was a trip where everything seemed to go wrong. We missed every single planned contact, sometimes by a matter of minutes. Our schedule was constantly being revised by Greg's quirks of behavior. We seemed to wander aimlessly through the country seeking prayer meetings or youth camps that were either not happening or just over by the time we arrived.

At one such youth meeting outside Budapest, we were informed that, although the meeting was over, there would be one the next day in Debrecen, which was three and a half hours away by car. Some of those present at the Budapest meeting were driving back that night and we could accompany them to find the location.

I climbed into the front seat of the car of Jenő Kopasz while his son Daniel sat in the back with his fiancée, Ildikó Széles. Jenő spoke not a word of English, but refused to recognize any such thing as a language barrier between believers. We talked all the way to Debrecen, occasionally helped by Daniel in the back seat, who spoke a little German.

Jenő told me of how God had called him to be a missionary to the gypsies years ago. He hadn't wanted to preach to the gypsies, who are a particularly despised people in that part of the world. But God insisted, and Jenő went from village to village for years preaching the gospel to the gypsies, eventually with quite astounding results.

That night in the car on the road to Debrecen, Jenő became my first real close friend in Eastern Europe. We would be close in both our friendship and family ties as well as in the work of the Lord for years to come. I would marry Ildikó's sister and Daniel would become my brother-in-law. My wife and I would later translate volumes of Bible study material and Daniel would found the first Christian publishing house in Hungary.

Of course, there was no way to know how that humble ride I shared would be so pivotal. If I had somehow missed that ride, I would have married someone else, had other kids, lived somewhere else for most of my adult life and followed another career.

Nor could I realize then that thirteen years, seven months and some days later, Jenő would die under my care in the hospital in Debrecen, the victim of a stroke. He would throw away his blood pressure medicine as a sign of faith, burst a vessel in his brain, and I would assist the professor of neurosurgery who tried to save him. His last words on earth as we wheeled him into the operating room would be would be to me: "She (the nurse) doesn't understand we don't fear death."

His funeral would be attended by so many thousands of believers from all over Hungary, Czechoslovakia, Romania and the Ukraine that the cemetery would not be able to contain them all at one time, let alone any single church building. In all my life I have never seen so many gypsies in one place, all clean and sober, dressed in their best clothes, to pay their last respects to a man as loved and respected as any on the face of the earth.

When we arrived in Debrecen it was late on a Saturday night. We parked the two cars outside a Unitarian Church building that the local Free Church rented once a week. A meeting was just breaking up.

At the Debrecen Free Church, it is customary once a month for people from small satellite churches throughout the country to gather for a big meeting that lasts the whole weekend. They call it *Csendes nap* or "peaceful day" and it consists of a Saturday and a Sunday wholly dedicated to the Lord and meditation on a passage of scripture, generally chosen by the pastor's wife. There is a weekly prayer meeting at which they pray for the Lord to lay the next month's scripture on somebody's heart and that passage is announced the following Sunday and spread throughout the church network. The pastor's wife usually gets the message from God. There is a saying in Hungarian that the man is the head of the house, but the wife is the neck and the neck turns the head. It was certainly true in this case.

Pastor János Marozsan was a man of incredible energy. When I met him that night he was thriving on a life that would kill most people. Like most influential pastors, he had long ago been removed from any officially allowed position as a spiritual leader. He worked in a factory. After work, he would come home, shower, eat a quick supper, hop in his little Trabant and motor off to some village in the area to hold a meeting or two. He had anywhere from 12 to 18 congregations at any one time to care for, and relied on the elders of the church to fill in for him. He was also the president of the Free Church Association, a loose conglomeration of evangelical churches that fit into no officially recognized denomination. How he managed the schedule for so many years is a mystery to me. I soon came to love and respect János as much as Jenő, and would work with him for years into the future until after the fall of Communism.

We were introduced around to lots of people who would later become my closest friends. Pastor János asked me if I would give a testimony during the service the following morning and I agreed. Then I rejoined Greg and Carla and we drove to the campground.

The next morning, we arrived early, but even then the

church was packed. We were given a seat on the platform with the rest of the speakers. On *Csendes nap* sometimes as many as a dozen lay pastors and leaders will preach in turn about what the Lord revealed to them through their prayer and meditation. The meeting can last for four hours or longer and is followed by a communal lunch, which is always delicious.

The Hungarians are nothing if not fond of good food. A famous Hungarian chef living in London was once asked what the difference between the English and the Hungarians was. He answered that the English live like kings and eat like pigs; the Hungarians live like pigs, but eat like kings. While I take issue with the "living like pigs" part, I heartily agree with the comment on Hungarian food.

Hungarians also love music. They break into song at every opportunity and church is no exception. There was a little band and anyone was welcome to sit in and play along. Many of their songs were written by members of their own congregation. There was no translator for us and as the service wore on Greg began to nod off. I was enthralled by the exotic sound of the Hungarian language. Many linguists believe Hungarian to be one of the most difficult of all languages. I wouldn't disagree. It has a vast literature, huge vocabulary and a complex grammar with forms not found in English. But it is one language that is worth learning just to appreciate its treasures. I never tire of its complexity, its richness and its sheer beauty.

When it came my turn to speak, a translator who spoke German had been found for me. She was a tall, well-proportioned raven-haired beauty, modest but poised,

talked me up to her sister and mother, making my welcome that much warmer. I don't know what I liked more about this place: the food, the language, the beautiful girls, or the friendly people. I knew in any case, this was a place I could live and love for a very long time.

We left the next morning for Czechoslovakia, the next stop on a grand tour which also included Poland and East Germany. Greg was getting more and more grouchy for some reason and it was becoming clear to me that he did not live in the same world with the rest of us. Although he had traveled extensively in Europe for years, he seemed to have a lot of strange ideas with no basis in reality, but from which no amount of persuasion could sway him.

One of his delusions was that Debrecen was home to the world's largest Egyptian museum. Both Carla and I expressed our doubts and he took offense and decided to show us. He drove us up one of the main boulevards of Debrecen, at the end of which stood a huge edifice clearly indicated by a sign on which was written "Kossuth Lajos Tudományi Egyetem." In Hungarian it means "Louis Kossuth Science University" but somewhere in the dark reaches of Greg's brain, he recognized that the first three letters of "Egyetem" (university) corresponded to the first three letters of "Egypt" and based on that had put together the whole idea of the world's largest Egyptian museum being located in Debrecen. The existence of a big building and three letters on a road sign were all the confirmation he needed to prove his point beyond all doubt.

This and other examples led me to seriously mistrust

his judgment and I began to wonder whether traveling with him might not involve just a little more danger than I was prepared to expose myself to. At least our last trip together ended on an amiable note and we remained friends despite our disagreements, always remembering the good times and never stirring up the bad feelings that came from unfortunate incidences.

One of the hazards of Bible smuggling was that we almost invariably got on each other's nerves on long trips under trying circumstances. The stress, the limited living space and the differences in personality that would normally cause no problems commonly surfaced creating friction among team members. Sadly, sometimes friendships broke up never to be reconciled over some relatively minor disagreement or differences in viewpoint.

On the other hand, there were also friendships forged of such depth and strength as to last a lifetime.

CZECHOSLOVAKIA

Liz was a tall, good looking blond from Pennsylvania who, with a story disturbingly reminiscent of my own, had been recruited on the promise of heading up the mission newsletter. She was a journalism major in college and wanted to get some real world experience. The school newspaper was too small time but she wasn't ready to put in her application to the Washington Post just yet. Over the summer, she would do some courier work and then ease into the writing job.

As it would eventually turn out, Paul never had any intention of letting her work on the newsletter any more than he intended for me to head up the mythological Bulgaria project. In fact, there were a half dozen of us there expecting to do jobs that never materialized and all of us eventually ran out of patience and went back to the States to pick up where we left off. It was the consequence of one of the mission's financial dilemmas. The summer missionaries brought in money to support the mission, so they needed to find something for us to do even if no need existed.

Marsha was in a little different situation. She had no plans for working with the mission for very long. She wanted to make a few trips and then get back to college in September.

She had no reason to knuckle under to any mission policy she didn't like or to abide by policies she disagreed with. She could and would leave anytime she wanted to.

That worried me a little. I didn't know her at all and did not want to find myself in the middle of a difficult situation in Czechoslovakia to have her suddenly quit and go home.

What made me even more nervous was that she had recently returned from a trip on which, word had it, she had caused some trouble. It was said that she wouldn't follow the leader's orders. I knew the leader, Gerry, to be neither unreasonable nor a harsh taskmaster. But rumors often have a way of misrepresenting the truth. I needed to hear Marsha's side of it.

"How was your trip with Gerry?" I asked Marsha. I suspected a personality conflict. Two more opposite personalities than Gerry and Marsha couldn't exist. Marsha was a head-strong, self-confident, outgoing, talkative blond of Slovak extraction with relatives in the country we were about to visit and who had traveled extensively both in the Soviet Union and in Europe before joining the mission. On her first trip of the summer, she had been put on a team with Gerry as the leader. Gerry, though having traveled in the East before, was a mild, quiet sort of guy who lacked any leadership potential whatsoever. He was nice enough, but may have gone a bit overboard separating women's tasks from men's tasks.

"You mean 'Peter-beater,'" Marsha answered.

"What!?"

"Oh, come on. Everybody knows his problem. He doesn't know how to sweet-talk a girl, so he tries to order her around and then when it doesn't work he goes home and beats off. Personally, I don't care what he does after hours as long as it doesn't involve me."

"Okay, okay," I interrupted. "So, what about the trip? I heard there were some problems."

"Not problems. Problem. Masculine singular," Liz interjected.

Marsha: "Yeah, he seemed to think he was God's personal advocate for Dark Ages religion. Women should do all the cooking and washing up. Men should do only 'men's work,' like…"

Liz: "Picking noses, watching TV…"

Me: "Liz!"

I could see this trip was going to be anything but dull. Marsha continued to pour out a stream of vituperation, got side-tracked into talking about the time she found bobby pins at the main department store in Moscow, and finally ran out of steam commenting on what was wrong with Aeroflot, the Soviet Airline.

"Alright, then. Let me bounce this off the two of you," I began, trying to get back to the reason we were together. "Marsha, we are both going to depend heavily on you for the language. Also, you know the culture better than either Liz or I do. We can all drive, so I suggest we share that equally. You both know that I can't tell you all the details of what we are going to do, but I'll tell you as much as I can and not make any important decisions without us discussing it together. Nevertheless, the mission holds me responsible for this trip and the final decision has to be mine. Can we all live with that?" There were nods from both. "We take turns with the driving, cooking, cleaning, etc. with no deference to gender. Equal pay for equal work."

"How about no pay and no work? I got the 'no pay' part down," said Liz.

"What I meant was equals all the way around."

"One for all and all for one!" said Liz, pulling out her pen and holding it up like a rapier.

"E pluribus unum," seconded Marsha.

"Like the three musketeers," I added, stuck for an appropriate phrase, but crossing my pencil with Liz's pen.

"Or Moe, Larry and Curly," added Liz, never stuck. "Woop, woop, woop..."

"Okay, then. Tomorrow I go up to Ermelo to get the car and talk to some people. I'll be back by evening and we'll leave the following morning. Anything else?" I asked in conclusion. There wasn't.

"Then I have just one question, Marsha," I continued. "How did you find out about Gerry?"

"Oh, it's a long story. It all started with Ken and Carol," she said. Ken and Carol were the only two married summer missionaries. "Ken and Carol pray for us all every day and they're praying for a wife for Gerry."

"Better to marry than burn," Liz pointed out.

"Seems like a good idea," I put in. "But I mean about the…you know."

"The masturbation?"

"Yeah. That." In the communal men's sleeping quarters we all could hear rhythmic noises and heavy breathing coming from Gerry's bunk every night, but nobody ever mentioned it.

"Carol told me. She and Ken can hear him through the wall." That was true enough. The wall was thin. I could occasionally hear Carol and Ken making love through the wall, too. "Obviously, he needs a wife."

"Or a milking machine. But wait. It gets even better. Tell him the rest, Marsha," Liz continued.

Marsha: "Well, the Holy Spirit revealed to Ken who that wife is going to be. Take a wild guess."

Me: "Bo Derek?"

Marsha: "Close."

Me: "Linda Lovelace?"

Liz: "Closer."

Marsha: "Me!"

I burst out laughing. "You mean Carol took you aside and said something like, 'Marsha, I just met your future husband. By the way, he's definitely not impotent.'"

"No, no. Carol told me about Gerry when Ken got his 'revelation.' Then Ken told Gerry the wonderful news and decided to just let nature take its course."

Liz: "That was before the trip."

"Sounds like a match made in heaven. Tell me, does Carol know Ken is nuts?" I asked.

"Yeah. But she loves him anyway. You know, she confides in me because I can keep a secret. Did you know that Ken gets 'revelations' all the time, and usually shares them at the Holy of Holies?" said Marsha.

The "Holy of Holies" was a snide term used by us ordinary summer missionaries for a prayer circle that was by invitation only and consisted of a small group of self-proclaimed baptized-in-the-Spirit prayer warriors. Next to praying, their favorite activity was that age-old Christian pastime of gossip disguised as loving concern. The gossip was commonly prefaced with a remark like, "I'm only telling you this so you can pray more specifically."

The only obligatory prayer meeting at the mission was the one that started the day and was held a half hour before breakfast at the Farm. The only members of the mission who never attended were the president Paul, his wife Millie, and the chief of operations, Jan. It looked to us summer swine as though the leadership was too important to pray with us and the Holy of Holies too righteous.

There was also a theological vacuum which resulted in a lot of indecision over precisely what we should be carrying into Eastern Europe. For example, it was easy to bring Bibles but not rosaries to the Catholics. But it was hard to decide what set of systematic theologies we should be delivering to the Protestants when requested.

Into this vacuum were swept the most fervent of our number, who were without exception Charismatic. The only argument one can pose to someone who claims to get his information directly from the Almighty is to compare it with Scripture. This, of course, demands a consistent Scripture-based theology and that was what the mission lacked.

"So has God shared with Ken anything we should be aware of before we invade Czechoslovakia?" I asked, not seriously expecting an answer.

"Oh yeah. You, Mr. Team Leader, are disobedient and need to submit," said Marsha.

"Yeah?" I said, getting interested. "How so?"

"Remember when you had that little disagreement with Ken over whether there are apostles today?"

"Uh huh."

Marsha: "That was a sign that you are disobedient and need to submit."

Liz: "Better submit. I think he means it."

"Let me get this straight. I'm supposed to submit to Ken?" I said incredulously.

"No, just to the Holy Spirit."

Liz: "But Ken will accept your sword by proxy. If you have an appointment, that is. How does next Tuesday look?"

"Look, not that it matters, but where did Ken get the idea about modern day apostles anyway? It's nothing to get this huffy about," I asked.

"Because Greg claims to be an apostle," answered Marsha.

"Greg? An apostle?" I said. "That's really a reach."

Liz: "The Fruit of the Spirit himself. And the term is 'reach around.'"

Marsha: "It's really bizarre. Here's a secret exclusive prayer meeting for super-saints led by a queer which dispenses the will of God on us lesser beings by making matches between unmatchables. I wouldn't marry Gerry if he were the last man on earth. Just being near him gives me the creeps. Ooh!" She shuddered for effect.

Liz: "Greg's still unspoken for. And you'd get an apostle who is guaranteed not to chase women to boot."

"Greg isn't a homosexual. He's just a little…effeminate," I objected.

with Piet, who was very interested in the fact that I had got myself into the Debrecen Atomic Research Institute. He wanted to know if I could do it again. I assured Joop that I could.

It sounded like, at long last, it would be the real thing. A real world clandestine assignment gathering intelligence right under the noses of the Communists! Although I knew well the possible consequences of getting caught, I had no fear at all. The excitement of finally getting to butt heads with the bad guys was a real rush. Like the night before a big game, I felt ready and confident and was itching to get out on the field and play.

The next day we made the long haul to Vienna and House Edelweiss, which by now had become a favorite stop-over of mine. You could always count on a welcome, hot water, good food and a good night's rest. They were wonderful people, those who worked with Toronto Christian Mission.

After breakfast the following day we left Austria and crossed into Czechoslovakia at the ancient Hungarian city of Pozsony, or Bratislava, as it is known today. Bratislava is a beautiful city on the Danube with a quaint old inner city dating back centuries. We were to meet our first contact, Mr. Krutschmeri, that evening and had time to kill until dark. We found a campground, staked out our site, drove back into town and spent the afternoon walking around with Marsha as our guide.

The inner cities of ancient towns like Prague and Bratislava are fascinating places. The pavement stones may date back a thousand years and the buildings are centuries old. There are interesting shops, houses and pubs everywhere you turn.

Czechoslovakia is as famous for its beer as Switzerland is for its watches and there are just as many varieties. Most small breweries, which are usually family concerns dating back hundreds of years, have a pub in the nearest town as a public outlet for their product. On Marsha's advice we had our supper in one such pub, which was actually a cozy little cellar with brick walls and low arched ceilings. It was dimly lit by electric bulbs and supplemented by candle light. Old casks, bottles, and farm tools lined the walls. We sat on polished hardwood benches at a matching table. Marsha ordered up some sausage, dumplings and pickles with a half liter of sweet, dark beer for each of us. We enjoyed ourselves for an hour or more before it got dark and then left to find our contact.

Mr. Krutschmeri was an elderly man, a grandfather but in robust health who exuded both wisdom and warmth. He lived up the stairs in an apartment block with his son, daughter-in-law and his grandchildren. We climbed the stairs, Liz and I tip-toeing cautiously while Marsha nonchalantly clip-clopped in her wooden-soled clogs. James Bond, she was not.

Without knocking, we entered the door of the right apartment quickly where we were immediately greeted by Mr. Krutschmeri himself. He had just come home from work; our timing was perfect.

I greeted him in German, including the password I had received, and smiling broadly he greeted us all in return. Marsha took it from there.

Tea was brought and cookies. We chatted in the parlor and I found out that he was a devout Catholic who rose every morning at four and spent three hours praying in church before going to work. He had also had some trouble with the police, which he dismissed as "trifles." I knew he had spent years in prison, so the expression "trifles" probably only emphasized his contempt for any effort the authorities might make to alter his behavior.

After about a half an hour, he asked me whether I would like to take a little walk with him while the girls talked to his daughter-in-law. As we walked the dark streets of Bratislava, he shared with me that the printing press was already in operation in Brno and that I could see what it was producing if I liked. I said that it would probably be best for us all if I didn't get too close to the place where it was operating and that I really needed to know what other material we could bring them that they weren't printing.

He stopped, looked me in the eye, and said, "I'm glad you said that. If you had showed too much curiosity about the press, I may not have trusted you further. We have to be very cautious these days."

I understood.

The next day we drove north to the town where we were to meet Jiri. The weather was pleasant and the Slovakian countryside beautiful. We passed through villages like the ones my grandmother must have been born in. The rolling hills were capped here and there with pear or apple orchards. There were horse carts on the streets hauling hay or manure. I wondered idly whether any of the peasants we passed along the way might be my blood relatives. My grandmother came from this area.

We arrived in Jiri's town just before noon.

This time I did not want the girls in on my business with Jiri. In fact, I didn't even want them to see me transfer the manuscript into the secret compartment in the Lada. I sent them off to walk around the town and meet me in about a half an hour.

Finding Jiri's apartment was no problem but Jiri wasn't home. Only his wife and baby boy were there, neither of whom I could converse with very well.

Jiri's wife greeted me, but did not smile. She was clearly distraught and on the verge of tears. She kept repeating that Jiri was in the "nemoshnitsa", whatever that was. Dredging the Slavic pools of my brain, I put together that "ne" is a negative prefix and "moshna" is a root word meaning power or strength. The "itsa" is a suffix for place. "Place of no strength" jelled in my mind to mean "hospital" or "sanitarium."

"Kde je nemocnice?" I asked in bad Slovak. She told me the town's name, which was about twenty minutes away by car. She drew me a little map and wrote the address, building and room number on it.

"Kniga? Papiri?" I asked expectantly, hoping she might know of the manuscript and be able to give it to me. She only shook her head and said something to the effect that she didn't know anything about any book or papers. It wasn't surprising.

I walked back to the Lada, meeting the girls on the road by chance. I explained to them that we had to drive to a nearby town and somehow get into a sanitarium of some kind to meet this Jiri.

We drove to the town and found the sanitarium easily. It was like a large bourgeois estate of about two acres just off a main street and enclosed by high concrete walls with a high gate at the front. There was a guard and a reception booth at the gate, but people were coming and going regularly.

The girls and I sat at a table outside a little cafe and had some juice to drink while I tried to think up a plan. I was almost completely at a loss for what to do, so I decided to walk up to the front gate and see whether I could just go in and look around. I could always pretend to be a lost tourist if the guard got suspicious.

There were people lolling around in front of the gate, talking and took no notice of me. I slouched against the wall and pretended to read a Slovak newspaper. Things were pretty casual and the old fellow manning the reception desk didn't look like he took his job too seriously. Inside the compound I could see what must have once been a nice place to live with green lawns, shade trees and several small two-story buildings. From the sketch map I had, I guessed at which one should be Jiri's.

Suddenly, as I stood there contemplating my options, a cloud covered the sun and it began to rain. Big heavy drops fell at first. Then it poured.

Everybody ran for cover and I put the newspaper over my head and dashed through the gate with no one paying any notice. I ran all the way to what I thought was Jiri's building, jerked open the door and ducked inside.

There was nobody there and a staircase rose before me.

According to the map, he would be upstairs in the room at the end of the hall. I quietly tip-toed up the concrete stairs.

At the top there was a hall and a door at the end of it. I heard the sound of talking coming from one of the rooms and prayed to God that they wouldn't look out to see who had arrived. I walked silently down the hall, tried the door which swung inward easily, and entered a three-man cubicle.

There was only one person there, lying on his bunk, dressed in brown and yellow striped pajamas. As he looked over at me, we both simultaneously experienced that witness of the Spirit and recognized each other as brothers in Christ. It was Jiri.

"Wilkommen, Bruder!" he said warmly.

"Jiri?" I asked. He nodded.

I explained how I had visited his house and his wife had told me he was here. He seemed in pain, and since this was a hospital of sorts, I presumed he was ill. I asked what was wrong.

Jiri pulled up his shirt and showed me the loose bandage that covered his abdomen. When he undid it, it revealed an ugly open sore penetrating deeply into the abdominal wall. Looking back now as a doctor I realize that it was a radiation ulcer, probably the result of cobalt treatment for a lymphoma. It looked like it hurt.

Jiri then asked how I managed to get into the place, guarded as it was. I had assumed that it was just an ordinary hospital, but Jiri proceeded to tell me that I was in a special place for special patients, most of whom were insane or

table with the waiter and their bags, leaving the coats on the counter.

"Do you believe in God?" I asked the old witch evenly, looking her straight in the eye.

"No. There is no God," she answered firmly.

"Well, you should, and you should thank Him every day that you live here. If you lived in my country, you would lose your job for talking to a customer like that."

"And if you lived in my country, we would sweep trash like you off the street and into jail where you belong," she shot back.

I swallowed back an urge to spit in her face and went quietly to my seat. I didn't need any trouble tonight of all nights. I soothed my burning ego with the reassurance that in a few days we'd be free in the West, but she would never know a better life than this.

There were a lot of jokes about the so-called "workers' paradise" as the Soviets liked to call their political experiment. One goes like this:

In school, the teacher asks little Ivan who the first man and woman were. "Adam and Eve, Comrade Teacher," he replies.

"Correct," she says. "And what nationality were they?"

"Russian, of course, Comrade Teacher," comes the confident answer from Ivan.

"And how do you know they were Russian?" continues the teacher.

"Because they had no clothes to wear, no house to live in, only one apple between the two of them, and they called it paradise," answers little Ivan.

In a lot of ways, though, it really was a worker's paradise. One could come to work late, leave early, and take time off during the work day. It was almost impossible to be incompetent enough to get fired. And, as our coat-check lady demonstrated, you could ignore or even be rude to customers with impunity.

But what made it a worker's paradise also made it a consumer's hell.

When darkness came, we drove over into the neighborhood where my contact was to be found. I gave Marsha and Liz the standard instructions to come back for me an hour later and drive down this road every half hour until they picked me up. If I'm not back by midnight, go back to the hotel and we'll meet there in the morning.

I found Peter's house in the darkness with some difficulty. I had to go around to the back door which looked out onto a small garden. I tried to walk right in without knocking but the door was locked. Peter heard the rustle of the door latch and after glancing out the window to see who it was, opened the door to let me in.

"Greetings from Brother Piet," were the first words out of my mouth. He became instantly friendly and welcomed me inside.

Peter had lots to tell about the changing situation with the underground churches, Catholic, Orthodox and Protestant. I listened eagerly. He spoke in a pedantic narrative, much like Piet had prior to my Bulgaria trip the previous summer, rolling out the long story of the churches under Communism, the progress in recent years culminating in the Helsinki Accords. Then he got to the really good news I had come to hear.

The Moscow Five were about to be released.

There were five Protestant pastors who had been holed up in the American embassy in Moscow for a long time. It was a three-way stalemate in which the U.S. had been unable to get them out of the country, the Soviets had demanded they be turned over to face the consequences, and the pastors refused to leave the embassy until the U.S. and Soviets agreed to allow them to leave the Soviet Union. No side had budged for months, but through the efforts of President Ford, a deal had been struck and they would be allowed to emigrate to the U.S.

It was what thousands of Christians had been praying for for a long time.

Before I left, Peter had another surprise for me. He gave me a long list of 126 names of Czechoslovak dissidents held in prison in violation of the Helsinki Accords. I should get the list out and give it to Amnesty International, but under no circumstances should it fall into the hands of the police.

"If they get it, I'm a dead man," Peter said.

With the list tucked away under my jacket, I left through the garden, entered an unpaved back street, circled around until I came upon the street where Marsha and Liz would pick me up and waited.

I waited for two hours, wondering where in the world they might be and what could have happened to them. Finally, in the darkness, I heard the brisk footfall of Liz approaching in the shadows on foot. Without stopping, she grabbed my arm and pulled me along.

"The police have the car!"

"What?! How did that happen? And where is Marsha?" I asked. Liz explained how they had gone back to the hotel, parking the car outside and went up to their room. They were downstairs waiting in the lobby just getting ready to come to pick me up when two policemen walked in wanting to know whose car that was. Marsha told them it belonged to her and Liz. They told her it was not safe on the street, and seeing two beautiful, single girls, became very friendly. They insisted on locking it up at the police station down the street for safety, and the girls could get it in the morning. By the way, they got off duty at midnight...

Fortunately, Marsha was more than up to the task of accepting their hospitality while turning down their advances. "I think she may have implied that she prefers girls," Liz speculated. Anyway, she was wise not to bring me into the picture, since it would have been a most inconvenient time to have to explain to the police what I was doing that evening.

We walked the long street back to the hotel arm in arm. Nobody bothers lovers alone late at night, and that's what we needed to look like.

In my hotel room, I decided that keeping the list of dissidents would be too risky. God only knows what might happen the following morning when Marsha went to get the car. I set about to memorize the whole list of names and in less than two hours knew I could remember them all long enough to get out of the country and reconstruct the list on the drive back to Holland. I tore up the list and burned it, piece by piece, in the ashtray and washed the ashes down the sink.

I would indeed get that list of names to Amnesty International along with the manuscript. Those, plus a similar list of names I would later bring out from the Soviet Union, would play a small part in the efforts of that organization to fight for the civil rights of citizens of Communist countries.

With that, we were over the worst part of the trip. We had only to meet with the priest in Lubina and we could go. The main reason for meeting this man had something to do with new laws the government were imposing on members of the Church, particularly the nuns. They were no longer allowed to be seen in public in their characteristic black and white habits, nor in any way to influence young people toward such a choice for their life.

Marsha's aunt was a nun, and Marsha's desire to visit her coincided perfectly with the purpose of our next contact.

We got the car without incident, checked out of the hotel after breakfast, and headed south to the town where Marsha's aunt lived.

It was a bright and sunny day, though large gray and white thunderheads patrolled the sky like battleships, both beautiful and ominous. We arrived at the town around noon, staked out a site in a nearby campground and left for the nunnery, arriving in time for lunch.

The convent was a large concrete and stone building at least a century old, somewhat dilapidated, but well decorated with flower beds and shrubs adding a cheery flush to an otherwise dreary setting. There was a small church next to it and a stone wall enclosing the entire complex quite similar to the asylum we had visited so recently.

Marsha's aunt and two of her friends greeted us warmly, and Marsha especially so. They hustled us inside for something to eat and drink, and immediately set to prattle in a rapid and very girlish manner rather out of place considering the dignity I expected of the order. Marsha had told us on the way down that they love to talk and always steer the conversation around to how to get her married as soon as possible.

In the rare bits of conversation that included Liz and me, I gathered that they were not happy about the new rules restricting the circulation of nuns in society. There was no indignation about the ban on proselytizing. God forbid anyone should talk any poor young girl into a life of celibacy without family and children. But it hurt not to be allowed to associate with others in the area as often as they had before. I'm sure each one of them had surrogate children and families all around town.

By late afternoon, I was ready to be moving on, but it seemed that the visiting was going to last a lot longer. I made a few hints that it was getting dark and we should be going, but the nuns were clearly reluctant to say good-bye so quickly. After all, with Marsha living in America, they might not see her again for a long while. Marsha herself suggested a solution, asking whether there would be any problem with her spending the night in the convent and us picking her up in the morning.

"You in a convent? You could use it," said Liz.

"We'll be by for you around nine," I said.

"Give Gerry some serious thought in the meantime," added Liz.

We bid Marsha and her aunt good-bye along with the other two nuns and struck out for the car in the darkness. We had parked a good half mile away for security and although night had fallen, I didn't think that finding it again would prove to be difficult. As we walked along, the sky, which had been threatening rain since we arrived, delivered on its promise. It was as though the clouds had burst and it poured like Niagara. Liz and I broke into a run, but we got soaked to the skin before we reached the Lada and tumbled inside.

Getting back to the campground also proved tricky. Neither the heater nor the defroster worked, and I had to vent the windows to keep the windshield from fogging up. I drove slowly but still got lost twice and we reached the front gate in just over an hour and a half.

Finding our campsite was easy and there were few other campers. Fortunately, the site I had chosen for the tent had good drainage. It was still raining hard and the wind had come up. Liz had kept pretty quiet the whole way, her arms folded around her wet windbreaker. She shivered in the cold.

"Look, Liz, I don't really want to put up two tents in this rain. With just the two of us, how 'bout we share one?" I suggested.

"F-f-fine with m-m-me," she replied.

I jumped out, opened the floppy trunk lid, hauled out one of the pup tents and put it up in record time. Then I grabbed two air mattresses and our two sleeping bags and heaved them inside.

"Come on! Let's get inside and blow up these mattresses," I shouted over the wind. She mumbled something in reply, sort of staggered out of the car and halfway fell into the tent through the front flaps.

"Hey, careful. We don't want to have to put this thing back up again," I said. She didn't answer, but just set about blowing up her mattress.

I finished first, undressed in the dark and hopped quickly into a nice, dry and soon-to-be warm sleeping bag. Liz finally finished and started to roll out her bag.

"Oh, no!" she wailed. "This thing is sopping wet!"

"Well, get Marsha's out of the trunk. She won't mind if you use it for a night."

Reluctantly, she pulled back the tent flap, crawled out into the storm and went to the trunk of the car a few yards away.

"It's s-s-soaked, too," she called back. The sleeping bags had been packed to the side of the trunk under the open crack of the faulty lid. In the downpour they had soaked up water like sponges. Mine had stayed dry only because I had packed it in a plastic garbage bag. Years of camping in the Pacific Northwest had taught me that.

"Well, come on back inside. We'll have to think of something else."

Liz slumped back into the tent, crying a little in the dark. I could hear her teeth starting to chatter.

"Geez, you really are cold," I said.

"I am not!" she snapped. "I'm just…freezing." After a

pause, "Maybe we could f-f-find someone…with an extra d-d-dry sleeping b-b-bag. Or maybe some hot t-t-tea or something…" She was getting irrational and incoherent. Not a good sign.

I had seen hypothermia once before and knew something about it. It's the greatest danger in a cold, wet environment. People die from it. And I knew what we had to do short of getting her to a hospital. It's in every first aid course I ever took.

"Alright, Liz. I want you out of your clothes and into this bag with me right now."

"I-I-I can't do that. I'll b-b-be alright…"

"Now!"

"But what would p-p-people think b-b-back at the mission?" she objected.

"Not half as much as if I had to take you into a Czech hospital or explain to your parents why I let you die over here. Now off with those clothes and get in here right now. I mean it!"

That was enough for her. She struggled out of her wet jacket and shirt, pulled off her shoes, socks and jeans and scooted over in with me, jerking at the zipper behind her.

"Hey, you've still got you're wet underwear on!"

"You don't?" she countered.

"Heck, no. They're wet. They'll keep us from getting you warmed up. They come off, too."

She paused silently for a couple of seconds and then in the tight sleeping bag tried to get free of her bra.

"C-c-could you reach these hooks in the b-b-back?" she asked. I tried with cold fingers to undo the contraption.

"Whoever invented these things should be shot," I muttered.

"You haven't had much p-p-practice at this, have you."

"No," I said, finally getting the thing loose. She pulled it off and flipped it over to the other side of the tent with the wet sleeping bag. "Hey, watch your knee!"

"Sorry," she said. "I'm just trying to get my panties off. It's too crowded in here." She was still shivering.

"That's the point. Well, be careful. I'm in here too, you know."

When she finally tossed that last piece of wet cloth out I told her, "Now roll over with your back to me and snuggle in as close as possible. I'll warm you up." I put my arms around her and pulled her in close.

"Hey! What's…"

"Relax and try to ignore it. It would happen to any naked guy in a sleeping bag with a beautiful, naked girl." I was trying to think of something mature and witty to say, but in my embarrassment couldn't, so I just lay there and tried to think about baseball. Finally I said, "If we had anything dry to put between us, I would, but we don't. Give me a break, okay? I'm trying my best not to enjoy this."

"Me too," she said quietly. She was silent for a while. "You feel good. Nice and warm," and she snuggled in a little more. She wasn't shivering as much as before. Then after a few minutes she asked, "Do you really think I'm beautiful?"

"Sure. Why even ask?"

"Cause nobody has said that to me in a long time. It was nice to hear it. You weren't kidding?"

"No, my dear. You're a scintillating epiphany of feminine pulchritude. The epitome of excellence. A double superlative. Can you handle it?" I said in a corny imitation of W. C. Fields.

She chuckled politely. After a silence she ventured, "Have you ever, you know, done it? I mean, I know you're not married, but…"

"No."

The conversation was leading in a direction I wasn't sure I wanted it to.

"I have," she said. Then she told me the story of how she had decided at age 19, to do it. She was heading for a career in journalism and wasn't planning on marrying anytime soon or on living a celibate life. Since she didn't want her premarital sex life to cause her unnecessary problems after she finally found her right man, she decided to plan it very carefully.

"What if it's important for your husband that his bride be a virgin?" I asked, interrupting the story.

"I wouldn't marry someone who couldn't deal with my not being a virgin. It's a double standard and I won't have any part of it. In our society, if a girl has sex before she marries, she 'loses her virginity;' if a boy does, he 'becomes a man.' If a woman does it, she's 'cheap;' if a man does it, he is 'experienced.'" She ended the tirade with, "I'm not a used car that loses value with the more experience I get."

"But it's sin," I objected.

"So is jealousy. And that's what this whole medieval rite is: institutionalized jealousy. Owning women like cattle belongs to the past along with with slavery. I'll marry a man who accepts me just as I am, like Jesus does, and treats me like an equal or I won't marry. I don't want to go through my whole life having to hide stuff from my husband."

"Okay, so go on with the story," I said, somewhat taken aback by the firmness of her very modern convictions. No wonder she had never ventured to say much around the mission staff. All the silly wisecracks and cornball comments were just a facade to hide what was deep down inside, a very serious and thoughtful young woman.

She narrated the whole tale of how she selected a thirty-ish divorced friend who had been sending all the right signals. They went backpacking up in Yosemite National Park one weekend and found an idyllic site where a river ran over a bed of large flat rocks, most of which were out of the water with the low level of the river in the summer. They made love lying on one of those rocks in the sunshine. After it was over, she revealed to him that it had been her first time. In shock he responded with, "Really? Are you hurt?" It hadn't hurt much, and the pleasure was what she remembered.

She turned half toward me onto her back and we kissed for our first time. "Are we going to make love, Mr. Team Leader?" she asked.

With a heavy sigh and some hesitation I said, "I don't think we'd better. God knows I want to, but we'd really be sorry afterwards."

"Uh-huh," she agreed, after a pause.

"Besides, explaining how you got pregnant might be harder than explaining how I let you die of hypothermia."

"I probably won't."

"Won't what? Get pregnant or die of hypothermia?

"Die of pregnancy."

"No."

She lay there in silence, the first time I had ever seen her at a loss for words. She finally commented, "You're right. We really need a little more time together first, don't we."

"And maybe a ring," I added. She turned back away from me and snuggled in close again. "Oh well. Making love in a sleeping bag in a Slovak campground wouldn't be that much fun anyway," I lied to myself.

"Are you sure you can sleep?" she asked. "I mean, I've heard guys can't sleep when they're excited..."

I laughed. "I'll sleep just fine. Now, good night, Liz."

"Good night, John Boy."

Wonder of wonders, I did sleep and dreamed wonderful dreams about swimming naked in the blue Caribbean and watching a beautiful girl on a sugar-white beach try to catch sea gulls and butterflies while I tried in vain to catch her attention. The girl alternately had the face of my sister, my mother and finally changed to Liz as I awoke to find my face two inches from hers, her mouth half open in slumber and a little drool running out the corner. Her breath smelled like cheese.

And for all that, she was beautiful. My first thought was to wipe the corners of my mouth and feel my matted hair and day's growth of beard. I must have looked ten times worse.

My second thought was that I had to urinate badly and needed to get out of the bag somehow to do it. I started to ease my way upward when Liz stirred. She opened her eyes, stirred with recognition and said with a stretch, "Good morning."

"How did you sleep?" I asked.

"Terrible. I didn't sleep a wink."

"Yes you did. I just saw you, and your snoring kept me awake half the night."

"I wasn't snoring. It must have been you."

"Couldn't have been me. I don't snore," I said. "Look, I have to find the boy's room. Could you let me out of here before I wet the bed? I've got to get my dry clothes out of the car and get myself to the nearest latrine." With that I rolled myself over Liz to the zipper side of the bag and let myself out. My left arm, which she had been laying on, was completely numb and buckled when I tried to put weight on it. I got out eventually. The morning air was cold.

"Is that a banana in your pocket, or are you just glad to see me?" Liz said in her best Mae West.

"I don't have a pocket and shut up or I'm telling Brother Andrew," I said crouching behind the flap and poking my head out to see if the coast was clear. It seemed to be.

"Ha! What are you going to tell Brother Andrew? That one of his top smugglers is a frotteurist?"

I made a mental note never to marry a journalist and then acquainted the Slovak campsite with the American tradition known as 'streaking' by a quick three-yard-dash to the trunk, fumbled with the keys, dropping them once, undid the wire, opened the lid, grabbed my suitcase and dove back into the tent. Liz was rolling on her back holding her stomach and shaking with laughter.

"Whew! I don't think anybody saw me."

"Better try it again," Liz suggested.

"That's enough out of you."

I pulled on a clean and dry change of clothes while Liz played peek-a-boo games pretending to be embarrassed and shocked. Finally, as I headed out the tent for the latrine she said, "You know what the real pity is? We'll both never forget this and we can't tell anybody about it. Well, maybe we can later."

"Much later," I called back over my shoulder.

We picked up Marsha and had a hearty breakfast, compliments of the nuns. We were on our way in less than two hours and made Lubina by mid afternoon. I probably would have told Marsha about Liz's and my adventure the previous night, but she was blissfully uninterested in our activities. Liz mentioned only that she had gotten the "King David" treatment when Marsha asked how we weathered the storm. The reference was completely lost on her and she continued to chatter on endlessly about her relatives and acquaintances in Slovakia and in Bend, Oregon, and getting side-tracked onto the virtues of the ski resorts in Bend over those in Sun Valley.

By the way, for the reader who on whom the analogy is also lost, Liz was referring to the incident at the end of King David's life when he couldn't get warm. His advisers thoughtfully found a beautiful girl for him to sleep with, sort of a human hot water bottle, though he didn't make love to her.

Our priest was easy to find and our visit uneventful, though friendly. Upon conclusion of our visit, we decided to push it to the border and spend the night on the Austrian side rather than stay one more night in Czechoslovakia.

The border crossing was relatively quick with the secret compartment going completely unnoticed. The wet camping equipment was the only thing that drew any attention from the border guards. Marsha drove through Austria as I sat in the back, reconstructing the list of dissidents from memory.

That evening we spent the night in a cozy little inn on the Danube just outside Regensburg where we had a hot supper of Wiener schnitzel and beer. I finished up the list of dissidents before crawling under a big, fluffy comforter and slept like the dead.

Marsha left for the States some days after we arrived back in Holland. The next time I would see her would be at the Neighbor's Fair in Portland, Oregon, some years later where she was helping her mother man the Slovak booth. I and my wife were manning the Hungarian booth.

Liz would get tired of waiting for her writing job with the mission to come together and leave disillusioned for America on the day I left for the Soviet Union.

I never saw Liz again.

OPERATION HEAVY BOMBER

Someone shaking my foot awakened me in the darkness of the men's sleeping quarters at the Farm. It was Joop.

"Operation Heavy Bomber is a go," he said. "You leave in the morning with Gerry for Romania."

I knew nothing of Operation Heavy Bomber. It was classified beyond my need to know and I had never even heard the name before. But Joop driving all the way out to the Farm at eleven o'clock at night to tell me personally rather than just phoning meant it must be important.

It was.

Joop briefed Gerry and me in his office behind locked doors while the rest of the Farm slept. Heavy Bomber was an elaborate and audacious plan to get over forty thousand Bibles into Romania at one shot. It involved Kor, a young Dutch truck driver with a family, driving his empty truck which had been modified to carry a huge amount of literature secretly into Romania to pick up some goods of some kind and dropping off the literature at a pre-planned drop site.

The plan called for a scout car to go in with people who knew the necessary information to make the drop. Kor, of course, knew nothing more than where to meet the scout car and how to get the Bibles out of the secret compartments. At the first rendezvous once inside Romania, I would get out of the car, ride with Kor to the drop site, arrange the details of the pick up, and then help with the drop. Gerry was along because he knew Kor, whom I had never met. I was point man for the operation because we were dealing with Saxons, a German-speaking minority in Romania, mostly members of the Brethren denomination.

The next morning we were awake early, fresh despite our little sleep. Mary packed us a box of food to eat on the way. Kor already had a day's head start on us, so we would be driving non-stop until we got to Cluj, where we would rendezvous at the Hotel International parking lot. We told nobody at breakfast where we were going, but an extra prayer was said for our safety. Everyone sensed it was something big.

We drove all across Europe, stopping only for gas and trading off on the driving every four hours. We crossed Germany and entered Austria late that afternoon, followed the Danube to Vienna and entered Hungary around midnight. Another six hours got us across that country. Crossing Hungary by night is faster than by day because the roads are relatively free of horse-drawn traffic then. The sun was coming up when we entered Romania and within a couple of hours, tired and in need of a cup of hot coffee, the "Cluj Cannonball" pulled in at the Hotel International.

We parked the car, got out and stretched our aching joints, then wandered into the restaurant for some breakfast. Gerry spotted Kor even before we could order. He was a young, powerful-looking man with a boyish face, savoring a cup of coffee. He gave no sign of recognition.

Gerry and I passed on breakfast and just ordered coffee, paying as it was brought. We had taken only a couple of sips when Kor got up, and slowly walked out the door without even a glance in our direction.

When Kor had left, I gave Gerry his instructions. "Give us about five minutes head start before you leave. You'll probably pass us on the road long before we get to the drop. If anything is wrong, I'll wave a shoe from inside the cab as you pass us. Otherwise, just meet me on the other side of the drop as planned."

I got up and left, winding my way around the empty parking lot and, not seeing anything out of place, made for the truck. I got into the cab on the passenger side as if I owned it and shook hands with my newest friend, Kor. He was friendly, but had an intensity that showed through. As we drove out of town, watching the mirrors for tails, he told me the story of how he had come up with the idea for "Heavy Bomber" three years before. It had taken that long to modify the truck and get the underground network in place. And of course he had to wait for an opportunity of pick up something in Romania. In this case, he was to pick up a load of canned strawberries in two day's time at Timisoara.

Kor knew nothing of the details of the underground operation in Romania, but suspected, as did I, that the mysterious Brother Piet was behind it. It had to have been set up by someone who had the brains, contacts and trust of some very important people within the Underground

Church in Romania. I couldn't think of anyone else who could have possibly put such an operation together.

It wasn't long before Gerry passed us. I kept my shoes on. So far, everything was going according to plan.

That was about to change.

As Gerry disappeared in the distance, I explained the basic plan to Kor. I would show him the "go" signal, and the drop site before he let me off to be picked up by Gerry again. He would wait while Gerry and I made the necessary contact and we would meet at the drop site at twelve midnight that evening to unload the Bibles as fast as possible. If the "go" signal was not in place, he should meet me the next morning in the square near the big church in Sigisoara, the nearest big town. I didn't tell him that our contacts lived in Sigisoara and if necessary, they might be able to contact him in the event of my arrest.

I scrutinized the map as we neared the road on which lay the drop site. Before the turn-off I spied a perfect spot for the "go" signal. It was a post near a tree line not far from the road. I could draw the signal on it while appearing to make a perfectly explainable "rest stop" in the bushes. Two horizontal chalk marks on the post would be Kor's signal to proceed to the drop site. Any other signal or no signal at all would mean to abort and try to meet me or Gerry the next morning.

We pulled off onto the road that led to the drop. It was a winding road through the Transylvanian hills, flanked by trees and having very few houses visible from it. It was perfect. Gerry and I both had a Xerox copy of a Polaroid shot of a sign by the side of the road that should be just before the turnout that would be the drop site. Besides that, the site was described in detail and the exact distance from the turn-off to the nearest hundred meters had been given us. Kor spotted the sign first.

He slowed down to negotiate the curve and around the bend on the left we saw the turn-out. Beside it was a small clearing surrounded by thick forest. Again, perfect.

"Think you can find this at midnight?" I asked him.

"I can find it in my sleep," he answered. It was meant to be funny, but neither of us was in the mood for levity.

Beyond the clearing about a half a kilometer we saw Gerry by the car, trunk open and tire-changing tools out on the roadside. Kor pulled over, let me out and, seeing no other traffic, ventured a wave and a thumbs up before driving off.

The "flat tire" was, of course, only a ruse to make my stopping to help look natural. We quickly stowed the gear back in the trunk and hopped in. From there we made for Sigisoara and our contact's house, the address of which only I knew.

At this point, perhaps a little digression is in order. As I have already alluded to, the mission, and indeed all the Bible smuggling missions operating in Eastern Europe, had been coming under increasing opposition recently. We had lost more cars and literature and had more couriers interrogated in the last year than in all the previous years combined. In the interest of learning from our mistakes, Paul had done his best to debrief those who had been caught and recorded the interviews on tape. In fact, he had been caught himself and was on one of them. The cassettes, needless to say, were closely guarded and very few people were allowed access to them.

When I came on staff, one of the things I was asked to do by Joop was to review the debriefings and make whatever constructive comments I could from the viewpoint of a trained interrogator and intelligence collector. It was immediately obvious to me that the police were using some well-known interrogation techniques. If one recognized the technique, one could counter it successfully, so I wrote up a small manual for training Bible smugglers in counterinterrogation. It soon replaced the previous training on what to do if one gets caught, but not without some resistance.

Jack was in charge of teaching smugglers how to behave if caught and his course pretty much consisted of lectures in what to say if they ask you a certain question. Example: If they ask you, "Do you have Bibles?" you should answer, "Yes, I have a Bible at home." I personally considered the instruction to be worthless, mostly because the KGB isn't likely to stick to Jack's script. What do you do if they ask you a question you don't have a cute reply to? Moreover, it was based on naiveté and waffling over the question of whether Christians should actively try to deceive the enemy.

Jack said he liked my manual but it could probably leave more room for the Holy Spirit to work.

Related to the debriefing tapes was the assignment of reading all the latest literature written by Bible smugglers. Quite a lot of books were being printed in the 1970s by people who had in some way been involved in helping the Underground Church. Some of them were elaborate stories of perfectly inconsequential trips. Others were gross exaggerations of an exciting event. One such book was written by an English lady who had visited Albania, got picked up by the police for leaving tracts on a bench and warned not to do it again. She made it out to be that she had been threatened with execution the next day. Perhaps she had been threatened and perhaps she believed the threat, but the idea that a British tourist would be hanged for leaving tracts on a park bench was clearly ridiculous, even for Albania.

Even more exciting was the book written by a Russian policeman who defected, found Christ, and had, by his account, persecuted the Church while serving with the Soviet police. It may have been true in large measure, but the account of his death in America was a willful fabrication by the editors to give the hero the obligatory martyrdom. It was said that he died of a bullet in the head and implied that the KGB had done him in to silence him. The facts, well known to all who knew the man, were that he had been sleeping with the pastor's daughter and shot himself in the head while playing Russian roulette with his own revolver to show off.

More sinister was the account given by two young Swedish men of their capture, imprisonment and interrogation by the Soviets. They had been caught with literature and were held and questioned for months until they broke down and told all. There were hundreds, maybe thousands of arrests as a result of two boys' ignorance of Soviet interrogation techniques. Their confessions were made entirely voluntarily and without duress, deprivation or threat of torture, a testimony to the effectiveness of interrogation techniques when applied by experts. I would later be sent to personally assess the damage and would find myself under KGB lights just as the Swedish boys had been. The damage they caused was immense. Whole networks were wiped out. Even worse, the book they wrote after their release revealed much information that could enable the Soviets to fight the Underground Church even more effectively.

Much of my first summer and autumn at the mission were spent reading these and similar accounts searching for ways to stem the damage we were doing by our well-intentioned efforts. On my first visit I had marveled at how easy it would be for the KGB to shut down the mission at Ermelo (or any place else) just by putting a man on the street in front of the Garage and taking down the license numbers of the cars that came and went, then sending all the numbers to the border stations. I casually assumed then that we probably just weren't important enough to bother. Later, however, it would become obvious that they were indeed waging a serious campaign to stamp out the Underground Church. Why they weren't doing a better job at stopping the Bible smugglers from contacting the Church was an unsolved puzzle for me then.

When the truth of the matter finally struck me, I was horrified.

But we'll get to that soon enough. Back to Project Heavy Bomber.

Heavy Bomber was a classic example of the two-pronged attack strategy we had adopted by the late Seventies. One car goes in with the information; the other, with the goods. The car with the information, or scout car, makes the contact, sets up the drop and leaves the courier car with the only task of leaving the Bibles (or whatever) at the agreed place at the agreed time. The locals pick up and distribute the literature.

The mechanics of the process are a little more complex and probably need a little elucidation. First, a drop site should be well concealed, little trafficked and perfectly natural looking. It should only be used once. The drop site we were using had been used before because it was so perfect, but I didn't know it at the time. You can't always do everything by the book.

Ideally, there should be a "load" signal and a "go" or "safe" signal. The "load" signal is a sign that tells the local contact that there is something (a message or some material) to be picked up at the drop site. It is located well away from the drop site and should be something natural like, for instance, a wad of gum stuck on the back of a street sign. For this operation there would be no "load" signal because I would initiate the pickup by meeting with our contact.

When the contact goes to make the pick up, he first checks the "go" signal, which the person who drops the message or material leaves. This tells the contact that the drop was emplaced and the person got away without being picked up and feels that the coast is clear for a pick up. Should the person be arrested, there will be no "go" sign. Some operations even allow for two "go" signs, one near and one far. This methodology for operating a dead drop is so standard that counterintelligence people would know to wait for the messenger to leave the "go" sign before arresting him. A second "go" sign farther away merely assures the contact that the messenger got away even after leaving the near "go" signal.

There is usually an "unload" sign left by the contact to show that the message or material has been safely picked up. For this operation, there would be no "unload" sign for us to check because after dropping the literature we would just get out of the country and Kor would continue on to Sigisoara for his strawberries.

With all this elaborate activity it is possible to run a really effective underground operation with minimal personal contact. Very few people can identify others in the network. Of course, this is not completely applicable to the Church, since the basis of the whole operation is usually on a close circle of dedicated friends who know each other. Nevertheless, it had its merits in keeping Western believers' personal knowledge of personalities involved in underground activity to a minimum. The sad fact was we were unintentionally betraying an alarming number of our believing brethren to the enemy.

Gerry parked the car off a main road in the center of town. He stayed nearby playing tourist while I went to make the contact.

The contact's house was actually several adjoining apartments with a central courtyard. It appeared that it was used as some kind of kindergarten or nursery. I walked in and asked the first adult I saw whether the man I wanted was available. As chance would have it, I was talking to the man's wife and she said that, unfortunately, he had just left that afternoon for a religious conference in Switzerland. I had missed him by less than two hours.

That was a minor disappointment, but since I also had an alternate contact, the project was still in no jeopardy. I asked the lady where I could find him. Since he was the assistant to the primary contact, I thought she should know that easily enough. By the way, the Brethren do not have pastors, but there are leaders in the church and these two were the equivalent of a pastor and assistant pastor.

She knew where the second man I sought was; he went with her husband to Switzerland.

Now my disappointment was greater. Both contacts gone and me with a load of forty thousand Bibles.

Fortunately, whoever set up Operation Heavy Bomber thought it important enough to install an emergency contact for just such a contingency. However, the emergency contact would be harder to find and lived several miles away in another town. We were running out of time. Just to be on the safe side, I asked the lady whether the third person I sought might perhaps have gone to Switzerland as well.

She had never heard of the man.

That is what makes a good emergency contact: anonymity. But it was also a pain to have to drive forty miles not knowing whether our contact was available.

Gerry and I drove to the next town as rapidly as we could. We found the contact's house without any problem, but there was nobody home. With some trepidation, I asked the neighbors, who fortunately were also Saxons and understood German. They directed me to the local church.

It was already getting dark when I got to the little Brethren church and walked inside. There were several ladies inside and some kids, but very few men anyplace. I greeted them and asked whether my man was present. One of the ladies answered with, "No. He is in Austria visiting relatives."

This time, I was crushed. We were only about four hours from the agreed rendezvous with Kor and I had struck out completely. I sat down and buried my face in my hands to try to think of what to do.

"Is there anything we can do to help?" she asked with genuine concern.

Taking a gamble, I pulled out half a broken comb and asked whether she knew anything about this. It was the recognition signal. The possessor of the other half of that comb would be my contact. She just gave a blank stare and said no.

With that, it began to dawn on at least one of the others that I had some very important business with one of their leaders. The other lady came over and said that there was a man in another town who might know what I needed to know. He was known to have had dealings with foreign believers before. But he would be hard to find and I didn't have much time. Besides, he was at best only a straw to grasp at.

I asked them to give me directions and draw a map, if possible, to his place. Three or four ladies sat down together and tried to get it right. After four sheets of paper and no agreement on how to get to the guy's place, a young man of perhaps 18 suggested a solution. He would ride with me as a guide.

That was immediately met with disapproval. It was against the law and the young man was a soldier on leave. For him the consequences would be especially severe if caught. I wasn't too keen on the idea, either. I already had some serious security breaks with at least a dozen people knowing that I, a foreigner, was urgently seeking certain people on secret business. But on the other hand, my only option about to be forced upon me was to abort the mission.

I decided to take a chance and go for it.

The three of us drove off into the Transylvanian night over winding mountain roads, the boy and I in the front, Gerry in the back. The sky was overcast and it sprinkled occasionally. We were about half way to our destination when a sight up ahead in the road made our blood run cold.

A police road block.

The officer waved us over to the side with a flashlight while two others walked around the car.

"Pashaport," he demanded.

They looked in at the three of us and I handed him two passports. He muttered something as he inspected the documents and I waited for him to ask for the third. I didn't know what I would say when he asked for it. Jack's stock question-and-answer list didn't cover this situation.

Then one of them at the rear of the car said something to the others. The officer at the window handed back the passports and said something to me sternly that I didn't understand.

"Sorry. Can't speak Romanian," I apologized. He pulled out a slip of paper and wrote a figure on it. It was a fine for a tail light out and amounted to about 75 cents American. I reached in my pocket, apologizing profusely that I didn't have any Romanian money and gave him a one dollar bill. He returned a gruff comment and waved us on.

"Whew! That was close," I said after we pulled out.

"You can say that again," said Gerry.

"Why didn't they ask for the third passport?" I wondered aloud.

"Maybe they just didn't see our friend here," Gerry suggested. A similar event had occurred in Bulgaria the previous summer to Tracy and me.

I asked our guide what he thought. He said that it was the end of the month and the police were stopping more cars to fine them for any little thing. Their paychecks were wearing thin.

"They didn't give you a receipt for the fine," he noted.

We were just starting to relax when we encountered another roadblock.

Again, one officer waved us over to the side while the others walked around the car.

"Pashaport."

Again, I handed him two passports while he looked in at the three of us. Again, one of them called out something from the rear. Again, they fined us 75 cents and I paid with a dollar bill.

And again they waved us on without incident.

We soon arrived in the town and our guide directed us to the church. I couldn't believe my eyes. There was some kind of prayer meeting going on and the church was packed. There were more cars parked around it than I had ever seen in any one place in Romania.

I would soon find out why.

I went into the church with my new young friend. As we entered from the back, one of the men on the platform immediately gave a smile of recognition and came down to meet us while the congregation continued to pray. We shook hands warmly and he took me aside.

"Do you know anything about this?" I asked anxiously, showing him the comb. He didn't answer, but simply reached into his pocket and pulled out the other half.

I almost burst into tears for joy.

I started to explain to him about the Bibles, but he silenced me with, "I know. That is why we are here. We are praying for Bibles and have gathered in faith that the Lord will send us as many as we can carry home."

That was why everyone had brought their cars.

They had no way of knowing I was coming that night. Indeed, had anyone known, one of our arranged contacts would certainly have been present. I'll concede that they might have known somebody someday would bring them a load of Bibles. Heavy Bomber had been under planning for three years. But I am sure they had not met like this every night with their cars ready for all that time. Events like this make it really easy to believe in the supernatural.

It reminded me of a story my grandfather used to tell. It was summer in Alberta and there had been a severe drought. The situation was so desperate that the local Indian tribes even announced they were going to do a rain dance. For my grandfather, the pastor of the local church, this was an Elijah opportunity: A chance to show his god answered prayer and the pagan gods don't.

He called a special prayer meeting of the congregation on a Saturday morning to pray for rain. When the congregation arrived, and after singing a hymn, Grampa stood up at the pulpit. He asked, "How many of you brought your umbrellas?" People smiled, thinking it humorous. Grampa was a jovial man fond of jokes.

Then he said, "Everyone without an umbrella, go home." Nobody had brought an umbrella and when it became obvious that the pastor was serious, they began to file out rather disgruntled. Grampa was left alone in the church to conduct a one-man prayer meeting with God. He hadn't meant to offend so many people, but the fact was that nobody really believed God would answer the prayer. By suggesting a little arbitrary demonstration of faith he had offended the whole congregation.

But he walked home in the rain.

I told my man that the Bibles would be at the drop site after midnight. Could he find it?

"Yes, in my sleep," he answered, echoing Kor's words.

It was too dangerous to risk a third encounter with the gendarmes, so we left the boy with the folks at the church and said good-bye. Gerry and I sped off to make our meeting with Kor. On the way back to the drop site, we didn't meet a single roadblock.

It was a little past 11:30 when we pulled over at the site. I did a quick recon of the area. It seemed clear. Then we jumped back into the car and drove up the road to the agreed "go" signal. I hopped out, walked to the post, scratched two chalk marks on it and ran back to the car.

We waited in the dark at the drop site for the quarter of an hour that remained. Very few cars passed us on the road that late at night and no police.

Then, at one minute to midnight, we heard the throaty rumble of Kor's diesel as he geared down to make the curve. Next we saw the glow of his headlights and then their full glare as he slowly rounded the final corner and pulled into the turn-out. He shut down the engine and all was quiet.

He got out and walked slowly in our direction. We got out and leaned against the car, looking as casual as we could.

"How's the food in Sigisoara?" he asked, initiating the password.

"All you can eat," I said, returning the "go" response. If I had said, "I've had better." Kor would have got back in the truck and left, dumped the Bibles somewhere and continued on to Timisoara for his strawberries, the mission a failure.

"Alright! Let's go," he said and we walked quickly back to the truck. Kor got up inside and started handing out packages. The Bibles were wrapped in plastic and taped securely. They were about one foot cubes weighing maybe twenty pounds each.

Gerry, Kor and I sprinted back and forth from the truck to the trees with packages of Bibles until we were sweating and out of breath. Twice it happened that a car drove by and we dove for cover. It took the three of us at maximum effort 45 minutes to unload the whole lot. Until then, I had not imagined just how big a load forty thousand Bibles is.

When we had finished, we put our arms on each other's shoulders, Kor said a quick prayer, and we left. Kor headed for Timisoara for his strawberries and we went to find a hotel.

It was not a happy hotel clerk that signed us in that night in Sigisoara, but we were two happy Bible smugglers when we finally hit the sheets after an almost warm shower. Even Gerry's usual pre-slumber activity didn't bother me. A little celebration was in order in any case.

We left Romania the next morning not even checking the drop site. "Never return to the scene of the crime" also applies to spy work. At my request, we spent the night in Debrecen, attending church at my favorite place. We booked a hotel, but I stayed over with my favorite family and caught up on things that were going on in Debrecen. It wasn't exactly according to the rules, but Hungary was the least strict of all the Eastern Bloc countries and one could stay in private homes if one registered the visit. Also, my future father-in-law was a prominent enough scientist that the police rarely bothered him even though he was a believer.

The ride back to Holland was uneventful. I would meet the man who had the other half of the comb again in December when he would tell me that they had gotten all the Bibles picked up and distributed in a single night. There had been no roadblocks and no problems. It was, all agreed, the single greatest coup in all the history of Bible smuggling.

Just how important those Bibles would be to the believers in that area, we could not fathom back then in

1978. But eleven years later, the believers in that area would assemble to protest the exile of a favorite and very effective pastor of theirs, the Reverend László Tökés. When ordered to disperse, they would do so only to reassemble in protest again. The police and the Army would open fire on them, killing dozens of men, women and children. The blood would flow until even the Army lost its stomach for the carnage and turned on their masters to spark the revolution which overthrew the tyranny of Nicolai Ceaucescu.

Thus would end the reign of the last Stalinist in Eastern Europe, executed in haste by his own people, shot by a firing squad selected from a heap of the names of eager volunteers, the chosen of which could not restrain themselves long enough for the "Ready, Aim, Fire" command to be completed.

Some whose sacrifice initiated the overthrow of that hated regime were believers who died with Bibles in their hands brought to them by three young men on a cool, overcast autumn night in 1978.

There is another reason why those believers, out of all the congregations in Romania, had the courage to take a stand to the death, but that I will explain in the final chapter.

THE SOVIET UNION

Shortly after my return from Romania, Paul informed me that I had been chosen to go on a trip to the Soviet Union with Luke Hanson, a guy from one of the California megachurches who had already made a couple of trips and spoke Russian. I had never met Luke but he had a good reputation and I was looking forward to traveling with him.

The purpose of the trip was confidential, involving the two Swedish boys from another mission had been caught on the Soviet border with literature, arrested and detained for several months. I remembered that they had been detained without charge and had eventually broken down and spilled everything they knew to the Soviets.

The boys had been neither tortured nor threatened nor even deprived of any necessities such as sleep or food. They had simply been separated from each other, allowed no information from outside save that which might serve to depress their morale. Each was told that the other had already broken down and told all and that when he decided to do the same, they could both go home. It was a variation on what is known as the "We Know All" technique. The prisoner is led to believe that the interrogators already know what they want to know and that acknowledging it is a mere formality and will do no further harm. There was also a mix of the "Emotional" approach because the sad letters from the boys' families were allowed in which further depressed them. Of course, the letters of encouragement or news of the public protests in front of the Soviet embassies were not divulged.

It appeared that hundreds of arrests had followed on the heels of the Swedish boys' confessions. Luke and I were going in to assess the damage.

There was also a printing press project the mission had tried to set up earlier in Kiev and we were to see whether that was still in action. I would also be taking in a few thousand rubles for financial aid to the believers in the Ukraine.

In the two months it took to process our visa applications, I worked closely with Joop on the intelligence files. Joop, a brilliant organizer, had taken on the monumental task of sorting and categorizing the hodge-podge of information that made up the history of our efforts in Eastern Europe. I brought to the effort a background in military intelligence.

Intelligence is a science and the gathering and processing of information is a profession with standards like any other profession. Information gathered can be categorized and organized to provide the user with immensely useful data. Admittedly, the military viewpoint has its limitations when applied to missionary work but it provided an excellent framework from which to start. Joop and I complemented each other well and made a great team.

Our major concern at the moment was crisis management

in certain areas. There was the imminent release of the "Moscow Five," the arrest of an important contact in Czechoslovakia, and now the crisis in the Ukraine. I knew about those, having done some of the field work directly related to them.

As I continued to work, I also found out that there was a crisis in Bulgaria but I wasn't supposed to know about it. Information is supposed to be compartmentalized so that only those with a need to know see it. But the Bulgarian crisis bothered me. I was supposed to be the future leader of the Bulgaria project and yet was forbidden access to this information.

At the time I still hadn't seen through Paul's duplicity but when I discovered that there had been another trip to Bulgaria after mine which had resulted in the whole network of seven underground pastors being wiped out, I realized that something was seriously wrong.

I confronted Paul with the information and asked him to spell out the Bulgaria project as he envisioned it, and to explain why I hadn't been informed of the follow-up trip into Bulgaria, much less been asked to participate in it. He said that they had decided to scrap the Bulgaria project and hadn't gotten around to telling me. Someone had reported that my Bulgarian wasn't good enough and that I had violated too many safety policies of the mission. Who that "someone" was and what those violations consisted of, Paul declined to say. It was only months later that I would find a more sinister force behind it all and Paul himself wasn't hiding anything intentionally. He was simply unaware of any facts concerning the matter but didn't want to admit it.

It embarrassed him further when I asked how that justified sending in someone who spoke no Bulgarian at all and managed to get the whole network arrested by violating mission policies. Moreover, it showed bad leadership for him not to take the matter of violation of mission policy up with me, or any other violator, personally before acting on the information.

I had grown to love those folks in Bulgaria, and the idea that at that very moment they were languishing in prison because of the carelessness of one of our missionaries, maybe even myself, sickened me. I wracked my brain to remember an incident where I might have been the one at fault. There had been times I might have been identified in the company of underground believers by the police. But a whole year had passed without incident and the recent calamity occurred immediately on the heels of the hushed-up trip.

I decided to talk to the lady who had led it.

She had attempted to take a letter out of the country, a direct violation of policy, and gotten it confiscated at the border. The letter led the police to the sender and thence to the rest of the network. When I asked her why she tried to take the letter out, she said that God had told her to do it and she couldn't disobey Him.

This added an emotional intensity to my efforts with Joop that I had lacked until then. If Bulgarians I loved were suffering in prison because of us, what might be happening to the Ukrainians I didn't even know yet?

And what other hidden skeletons remained in the mission's closet?

The more deeply I delved, the more sinister a picture

began to take shape. First, I tried to match the trips with the cars used and the people who participated in order to construct a general history of our efforts over the 1970s. I made a list of all the times on record that our people had been caught at the border or inside the target country. That was how I discovered that when a car was caught once, it tended to get caught again and again, despite being used in different countries. Obviously, the Warsaw Pact intelligence services shared information.

A more arduous effort was the reading of the after-trip reports written out by the participants. They tended to be long, hand-written, rambling, often difficult or impossible to read, containing little information of intelligence value, and generally disorganized. I decided that it would be best if I or Joop individually debriefed these people in the future for the sake of obtaining concise, clear, useful information. But despite the confusion, one phenomenon still caught my attention.

It was reported sporadically that at the border the police had found the hidden literature and done nothing about it. The guards looked right at the Bibles and yet let the couriers pass as though they had not seen them. The team would go right on in believing that God had blinded the eyes of the police to the literature and continue with the assignment. I began to wonder whether there was any correlation between such "miracles" and arrests of believers these teams visited. Perhaps the police were following the teams to the contacts' houses.

It was an important issue because some missionaries steadfastly refused to hide literature or attempt in any way

about it, he answered that he thought I had been joking and threw it away without showing it to anyone. It was a testament to my own stupidity that I saw him acting only out of personal spite toward me instead of what it really was. He had surreptitiously taken me off of the Bulgaria project, chosen an inappropriate replacement who had gotten the whole network arrested, and blocked a plan that would enhance security in the China project. He generally chose the teams and team leaders and was in charge of assigning the cars. He had virtually a free hand in running the operations of the mission any way he liked and kept Paul in the dark as to the details.

In retrospect, what he was doing is now so clear, but at the time I was too naïve, too self-absorbed to figure it out. I knew he didn't want me there, but just how badly and the lengths he was prepared to go took me completely by surprise.

Luke and I were walking into a trap.

Luke arrived from the States and while he rested up and got caught up on old acquaintances, I went up north to Groningen, a city in the northern part of Holland, Friesland actually, for a special element of our coming trip. There I met with an old Dutch cobbler who had specially prepared a pair of wooden-soled clogs for me. The old guy spoke no English, but we got on fabulously and he showed me how to take the rubber sole off the shoe and open a secret compartment he had carved in the right one. In the compartment, which could be resealed, was a roll of Russian rubles I was to give to whoever Luke told me to. I wouldn't know that information just as he wouldn't know where I had the money hidden.

Back at the Farm, Luke had already picked up the car, a blue Russian Lada which, to my dismay, had already been nabbed both in Czechoslovakia and very recently in East Germany. We were going to cross the DDR on our way to the Soviet Union, but since we wouldn't be using the secret compartment, it was deemed "safe" by Jan.

Luke was a Charismatic, though apparently not as far out as Greg. He seemed to have his head screwed on right and had made two trips to the Soviet Union in the past. He was about my age and in good shape. I looked forward to a good trip together.

We left early on a chilly October morning. Summer was gone; all but a handful of the summer missionaries had gone home and those who hadn't would be gone by the time Luke and I got back. "*If* we get back..." I thought to myself. The cold weather, the departure of some close friends including Liz who I was starting to love, and the dawning knowledge that we were about to do something so dangerous that no amount of money would have enticed me had left me with a constant feeling of foreboding. We were not just smuggling Bibles like a couple of well-meaning religious fanatics; the mission to seek out our underground printing press and the thousands of rubles in my shoe put us squarely into the class of felon under Soviet law. We were spies engaging in activities which destabilize the Soviet government and therefore, insurgents. They could easily send us to a very cold prison in Siberia for a very long time if we got caught. Indeed, such acts carried a potential death penalty, though realistically there was little chance of them applying it to us.

Still, anything could happen.

Luke was more enthusiastic than I to get started. He had friends to see where we were going much like I had my Bulgarians and Hungarians. He was anxious to see how they were doing. As we plied the autobahn towards our first night's stopover on the East German border, we listened to cassettes by "Abba", "Boston" and "Second Chapter of Acts." As was typical of someone from a California megachurch, Luke was personally acquainted with several celebrity Christians including members of the Christian rock group we were listening to. The "Second Chapter of Acts" was one of the most popular Christian rock groups in the late 1970s. They borrowed a lot from secular motifs which gave them a very exciting, professional sound. I liked the popular Swedish group "Abba" but my personal favorite was "Boston." They were doing some really innovative stuff with two lead guitars. Luke was the only person I met at the mission who could also appreciate the quality of music without feeling obligated to moralize about whether it was "Christian" or "worldly." There is a tiring attitude among some of my friends that music is bad if it is secular (unless it is classical music) or good if it has something about God in it.

We overnighted in Braunshweig in a Zimmerfrei, a private home with rooms to let by the night. At breakfast, we chatted with the lady who fed us and got the conversation turned around to religious things. Luke didn't speak German and tried his best through me as an interpreter to evangelize the lady but she just wasn't getting it. I really hate being used as an interpreter for evangelization. You never know what the evangelist is going to say or do and it has led to some embarrassing moments in my life. In this case it didn't come to that but I was still uncomfortable. I think Luke took it as a sign I was less than one hundred percent committed to spreading the gospel.

The border crossing was easy and quick due to characteristic German efficiency and the lack of summer lines. Whatever uneasiness I had due to the knowledge that this car had been picked up before was quickly dispelled when they waved us on through, our transit visas firmly in hand.

And right into a speed trap.

Just across the border there was a place where the speed limit suddenly dropped from 80 kph to the ridiculous speed of 20. Luke, who was driving, couldn't slow down in time and there were East German traffic police with radar guns waiting for us and no interest in our excuses. One of the officers simply wrote out the figure in East German marks and said just one word: "Bezahlen." We had only exchanged enough money for gas in case we had to fill up before we hit Poland and it wasn't enough. They took what we had, however, and left us effectively penniless. We hoped we could reach the Polish border before we had any more unexpected expenses.

Luke was also mentally flogging himself because it was the mission's policy for us to pay for our own fines incurred in the line of duty. It was a policy I strongly objected to because of the corruption in the East. There the police often fined us as Westerners for any convenient reason and occasionally we did have to break some curfew and traffic laws in the line of duty. I once got fined heavily in France for an improperly licensed vehicle which I was sent to drive to Holland where it would be modified to smuggle Bibles. Since it was the mission's fault, I only had to pay half of the fine. But I had to reimburse the mission the whole forty francs I lost when a Turkish vendor shortchanged me in a train station while waiting for the car to arrive. At least our fine in East Germany served to remind us never to let our guard down.

We made it through the DDR and into Poland without further incident and overnighted near the Russian border at a youth hostel. The place reminded me of an old YMCA with a gym on the ground floor. After the long ride, I needed some exercise, so I changed into my gym clothes and headed downstairs for a little recreation. Luke's low back was hurting him, so he stayed in the room.

In the gym was a lot of old, 1950s looking gymnastic equipment. I had been a gymnast in high school and thought this would be a great opportunity to rehearse some old routines. There were a bunch of Polish kids working out on the mats, so I thought I'd just go over and show them what Americans can do. While I stood there trying to decide what to do first, one of the Polish kids shot down the mat, did a round-off, back handspring and a double back somersault.

I left quietly hoping I hadn't been noticed.

The next morning we started early for the Russian border. I put on my ruble-stuffed shoes, knowing that on my feet would be the safest place for them. We knew that we would probably be there for several hours, even if there was no line. The morning was grey and dismal with the promise of winter in the air. It didn't take much to remind me that the armies of Napoleon and Hitler had both sniffed this air about this time of year while going in the same direction.

The land was mostly flat, wide-open farmland. There was mud and dirt everywhere, even on the road. It seemed that nothing was new or clean. It was like being transported back fifty years in time.

It is difficult to put into words the feelings I had approaching the Soviet border. I was well aware of the dangers that lay ahead of us, dangers that were punctuated by the carelessness of the mission in setting this foray up with a car that was already known to the enemy. I knew they would be waiting for us with information they had dug up while processing our visas. How much information, I didn't know, but there would certainly be a trained Soviet interrogator waiting to use every shred he had to his advantage.

Exactly like I had been trained to do in interrogator's school at Fort Huachuca just three years before.

Nevertheless, my feelings were not of fear or trepidation, but of resolve and a grim eagerness for combat. This would test my mettle as no assignment had thus far. I like to think of myself as a warrior, but there is no way to tell whether you have the stomach for combat until it is forced upon you. No amount of training, no shelf of shooting trophies, no green beret nor black belt can predict the way a person will behave in battle. I hoped I would measure up.

A fault common to warriors is that we crave recognition. Admit it or not, we like to show off, and showing off has gotten me into as much trouble as any of the other stupid things I tend to do from time to time.

It was about to again.

As Luke and I drove on in silence, I remembered the classes and exercises our instructors gave us on interrogation and the tricks they used to beat us when we tried to get all the information out of them. I learned how to build a plausible story using some of the facts and another plausible story around that one so the interrogator, if he didn't believe me, would have to peel away the cover stories like leaves on a cabbage to eventually arrive at the truth. I learned to beat a lie detector and to take pain. I knew how the Soviets work and had at times played the role of Soviet interrogator in war games. Now at last I would be meeting a real one. I wondered what my interrogator, my opponent, would be like.

Could I fool him? Could I beat him?

Long before we reached the Polish-Soviet frontier, there were warning signs that we were approaching the border. Then fences, obstacles and guard posts. This certainly wasn't the US/Canadian border. These brothers in culture and history didn't trust each other.

There was no line to speak of at the border, yet we were there for more than four hours. The guards searched our luggage and vehicle very thoroughly. We were escorted from counter to counter to verify our passports, our visas, exchange our money and get our gas coupons. Between each stop was a long wait which we filled mostly with walking around the car while the guards looked it over top to bottom, inside and out. They weren't inclined toward friendly chit-chat but neither were they hostile. If we offered them chewing gum they usually took it.

Finally, after several hours of this, we were ushered into the office of a very friendly Intourist representative. Although Intourist is the agency that manages tourists, it has an extra function in security and counterintelligence. The Intourist agent may often be a KGB officer or at least answer to one. He was the man I had been anticipating.

He was a slim, dark-haired fellow of about thirty with an open, friendly manner, but with eyes that didn't quite smile in unison with his lips. He was dressed in a suit and tie, but had a military look about him. He chain smoked.

We were ushered into his Spartan office and he half rose briefly to beckon us to have a seat in front of his desk. Luke spoke to him first.

"We have arranged an automobile tour of the Ukraine mainly to see Kiev..." he began.

The official interrupted him before he could finish with a raised hand and a head cocked and eyes narrowed in incomprehension. "Pa Ruski? Oder Deutsch?" he asked. "Ya harasho nye panemayoo pa anglisky."

Luke was slightly taken aback but nodded for me to take up the conversation in German. We had already agreed that neither of us would admit to knowing any more than a smattering of Russian.

"I speak a little German," I began. "We have arranged a trip through the Ukraine. Here is our itinerary." I handed him the papers.

"What is the purpose of your trip?" he asked after a glance at the documents.

"Just tourism. We would like to see some famous places," I answered.

"Such as..."

"Well, Kiev and Odessa. I hear Odessa is very nice," I continued.

"So is Florida," he smiled. "But why bother to come so far?" he pressed.

"It's not so far really. We were already in Europe and wanted to see something out of the ordinary. Besides, the Soviet Union is very cheap."

He seemed to accept that as reasonable and then asked, "What do you do for a living."

"We are both college students," I answered, sticking to our agreed story.

"October is a strange time for college students to travel. Shouldn't you both be in school?" he asked.

I had been translating all the questions and answers to Luke as he hadn't been able to participate up until this point. He wanted to get back into the conversation. "We met in Holland this summer and decided to travel together because I had been to the Soviet Union before and he hadn't..." Luke started to explain in English. The official just narrowed his eyes with a quizzical smile and interrupted with, "Deutsch, bitte, Deutsch." I amended the narrative a bit because I felt Luke was explaining too much that hadn't been asked. It looks nervous and can be taken as a sign that a person is hiding something.

"We've taken some time off school and will start up again in January. In America it's not uncommon," I said.

"But what did your friend just say?" our interrogator asked. He had caught that the translation hadn't been exact and wanted to let Luke talk some more.

"Gotcha!" I thought to myself. "You understand English and want us to think you can't so we'll talk freely to each other." I tried to think of some way to keep Luke from playing into his hands by saying something to me in English he thought the interrogator wouldn't catch.

Fortunately, Luke was too alert to fall for that. He continued with, "Tell him how we met in Holland last August and decided to try to make a trip to the U.S.S.R. together."

I did.

There were a few more questions about where we got the car (we rented it), how much money we were bringing in (a few hundred dollars), and whether we were planning on seeing any friends, relatives or acquaintances (no). Then, without warning he asked, "Do you believe in God?"

"All Americans believe in God," I answered in a way that would have made Jack proud.

"Yes, but do *you* believe in God?" he asked more intensely, pointing a finger at me.

"I do," I said. "See? It's on our money," and I pulled out a bill showing him where it is printed "In God We Trust." I hoped the non-answer and the harmless attempt at a bribe would derail that line of questioning. He didn't bother to touch the money, however, and kept right on track. I think he knew he was on to something.

"No one in this country believes in God anymore," he said. "Why do you?"

I tried to gain the initiative with, "But there are churches everywhere in the Soviet Union. Many of them are quite big and famous."

"But nobody goes to them except for some old people out of habit," he responded. "How about your friend? Does he believe in God?"

I translated to Luke, who asked, a little too excitedly, "Why does he want to know that?"

"I don't know," I said.

"Well, ask him why he wants to know," Luke ordered. "Is it illegal for a tourist to believe in God?"

I asked, in English, why the official wanted to know. All I got was a "Deutsch, bitte, Deutsch." It seemed I wasn't going to be able either to distract or rattle him. He was too cool.

"My friend asked why you want to know. Is it illegal?" I said in German.

"No," he answered simply. Then he stamped our papers, gave them back and sent us off to get our gas coupons. He wished us a pleasant journey, but with a smile that said he knew we were hiding something.

On our way to the gas coupon counter Luke whispered to me, "I know that guy. He was here when I came through last year. He spoke perfect English then, even with a noticeable New York accent."

"He's not just an Intourist guide, either," I added.

We got our coupons and started out to the car, but temptation got the better of me. I poked my head inside the interrogator's office unannounced and asked him in English, "If we run out of these coupons, can we get more somewhere else?

He had his head in a file cabinet and looking up said, "Yeah, sure."

I squinted my eyes, cocked my head and said, "Deutsch, bitte, Deutsch," and we both laughed.

I shouldn't have done that.

In a few minutes, we were speeding down the wide, Ukrainian highway through miles and miles of wide open spaces dotted by the occasional village. We had an itinerary that demanded that we be at a certain hotel in a certain town each night. No deviations from our route were permitted and if we got caught off the designated route it would certainly mean trouble. Of course, we planned a few deviations but we would have to be extremely careful.

There was nothing to do in our first town, Lvov, so we took a pretty young guide supplied for us by the Intourist desk at our hotel in our car and saw the town. We had plenty of time alone with her to ask her what she really thought of the Communist system. She only answered non-committally by saying she was not interested in politics and just wished that the politicians would leave ordinary folks like us alone.

Later in Odessa, we would get a big, stern, ugly Party member for a guide who loved to argue politics and was just itching for a debate of any kind. She was obviously disappointed when Luke and I showed a vast ignorance of the political issues of our day. The most amusing moment of our time with her was when we were approached by a young man wanting to know whether Luke or I wanted to sell our jeans. When I said I'd ask our Intourist guide whether that was okay, he blanched and hurried off. Our guide glared after him with the comment, "I wonder why that fellow isn't in the fields helping with the harvest like the rest of the boys his age."

Our next stop, Ternopl, had a contact Luke wanted to meet. He had been there before and knew both the man and how to get to his house. Nevertheless, we took a map along with us just in case. In our hotel, wordlessly in case of microphones in the room, we looked over the route we would be taking. It would involve only a bit of a walk, as it was not far from the hotel and we timed it to arrive about dusk.

As we stepped out of our hotel and rounded the corner Luke and I agreed on a handshake that we would find the house. It was an idea of Luke's based on a place in Scripture where if believers agree on something in the name of the Lord, it will come to pass.

The Lord must have meant something else because we never found the place. We walked and walked, each street looking familiar to Luke but turning out to be wrong. Luke's back began to hurt him from all the walking. People who have bad backs know just how much of a damper it can put on things without looking very serious to those who don't. The more pain he began to show, the more frustrated he became at not being able to find the house.

Finally, I suggested we take out and consult the map. He wouldn't do it because he didn't want anyone to see us looking for something and draw unnecessary attention to ourselves. Then he began to speak softly under his breath.

"What?" I asked, not having heard him clearly. He didn't answer me but went on mumbling. Then, as I listened closer, I recognized that he was praying softly in tongues.

"Luke, don't you think we ought to have a look at the map?" I proposed.

"Oo shara bashnaya krishnaya…" he continued.

"Look, there's nobody around now and it's almost dark. Let's chance a look at the map, okay?" I pressed.

"Kara bashnaya krishnaya, sashnaya…" he said, looking at me intently.

I didn't know what to do. Luke had flipped out and I hadn't the faintest clue of what we were looking for, so I just walked on next to him listening to him mutter and occasionally pound a fist into his hand. Finally, it just got dark and we had to go back. Luke was in a bad mood the rest of the evening.

There was a TV in the room, so we turned it on just to see what there was. It was some folk festival and a colorfully dressed lady was screeching out a song in some weird language. We looked at each other, Luke and I, and simultaneously said, "Gong!" and turned it off. That at least got us laughing again.

The next day was a long drive to Kiev. We would stay there for two days. We had two contacts to make, the most important of which was the pastor to whom we would give the money and inquire as to the status of the underground printing press. We decided to do that first.

In the car on the way, while Luke drove, I carefully went to work on my shoe. The highway was wide and sparsely trafficked. We had little fear of being pulled over, but just in case, I had a bag ready to throw the shoes into if we were unexpectedly interrupted by a police roadblock.

I covered my lap with a piece of newspaper to collect any splinters or other evidence that I had dug into the wooden soles of the shoes. Then, with a razor-sharp blade of my pocket knife, I separated the rubber sole from the wood to which it was glued. Under the flap was the thin wooden cover to the secret compartment held in place by four very short screws. I unscrewed these with another blade of my knife and the lid came off. I took out the roll of rubles and stowed them in my pocket. After this, I replaced the thin wooden lid, fastening it back in place with the screws. Finally, with rubber cement, I refastened the sole as best I could.

It didn't look completely professional, but would draw no undue attention. Without the rubles, the compartment could be felt as a soft place under the sole, but one would have to specifically look for it to find it. I wanted to keep the shoes in case we needed a place to stash some small piece of film or written information on the way out.

I should have thrown the shoes away instead.

We arrived in Kiev and found the hotel quickly. There had, however, been a change and we would have to move to another hotel. No explanation was given. At first we thought something might be up, but there were familiar faces in the lobby also being transferred to another hotel. In making a tour of the Soviet Union, only a small choice of preplanned routes were offered and it tends to work out that whole groups of strangers wind up coincidentally staying in the same hotels night after night, since everybody has to take basically the same trip. George and Sylvia Something-or-other from New York had been Luke's and my neighbors since Lvov. We didn't exactly know which of the faces belonged to them, but every night in the next room Sylvia played straight man to George.

"Ya wanna sendwich, George?"

"I wanna plane ticket outta heah, Sylvia."

or: "Ya ready for the circus, George?"

"I'm ready for the plane home, Sylvia."

It was already late in the afternoon by the time we got settled into our new place, so we decided to put off the money drop until the next evening. This evening we would go to a ballet (with George, Sylvia, and all the rest of the strangers) courtesy of Intourist. During the intermission, we would slip out, try to make a contact of Luke's and get back before the final curtain. We had enough time to scout the place out before the Intourist bus left the hotel.

We found the theater and drove from there to the vicinity of the contact which, fortunately, was reachable by tram. We could hop out of the theater, take the tram to the contact and back again in less than half an hour which would be plenty of time.

Parking the car several blocks away, Luke and I strolled up the street on which our contact lived. Luke knew the place. On the way he filled me in on the man. He was a Pentecostal pastor who, it was reported, was closely watched. We may not be able to see him and would have to be extremely careful not to be observed. He lived in a small house in a courtyard just off the street on which we were walking.

As we walked past the opening to the courtyard on the other side of the road, the only mildly suspicious thing we observed was a man with a German shepherd on a leash. It was most likely just a man walking his dog. We walked on, crossed the street further down and strolled back to get a better look at the courtyard as we walked by. The man with the dog was still there smoking a cigarette in the cold Ukrainian autumn afternoon. Luke and I glanced inside the courtyard as we passed, continued up the street, and turned the next corner on the route we would take back to the tram stop.

Rounding the corner, Luke whispered to me, "That's it! That was his place. I think we can get in if it's dark enough."

We found the tram stop, then headed back to the car and drove back to the hotel. We had just enough time to gobble a couple of rolls and some cheese and change clothes before assembling with the others in the lobby.

We dressed appropriately in suits and ties for the theater and wore long grey overcoats such as would not look out of place on the streets of Kiev in October. I had the roll of rubles in my pocket, thinking they would be safer there than in the hotel room. Besides that, I had a few items that might come in handy: my pocket knife, some wire, a penlight, a piece of red cellophane, a small plastic bag, a condom, an aerosol breath freshener, a small can of cayenne pepper, a cigarette lighter and a pack of American-made Camels.

One might wonder what possible use some of those items could be. The truth is, I would have liked to have included a hacksaw blade sewn across the shoulder of my suit jacket, a length of parachute cord, and a knife with at least a four-inch blade. If caught, however, such things would be as hard to explain as a hand grenade. I could only include items an innocent tourist might have on him.

A multipurpose Swiss Army pocket knife can come in very handy at times. Both a pocket knife and a source of fire are two things I am never without. The pack of cigarettes explains the cigarette lighter and can be as good a bribe as dollar bills. Wire is useful if you need to repair something fast or tie something up. A penlight is to see name plates in the dark or read a map. The red cellophane makes the beam less noticeable in the dark. Plastic bags keep paper dry and a condom is the perfect thing for storing a roll of film. The aerosol of mint fragrance and the pepper were for self-defense, both of which sting if introduced into the eyes or nose.

The Intourist guide assembled us, counted us and gave us each our tickets. We would be randomly seated, I was happy to see, and she said that we should meet in front of the theater as soon as the performance was over.

Perfect.

At the theater, we checked our coats and found our places well before the performance started. The theater was only about half full. Luke and I lost sight of our guide and hoped she had done the same with us. The performance was a weird locally-written play filled with Communist symbology crushing the superstition of Church symbology. Neither Luke nor I paid much attention. Our minds were on our impending sortie.

At intermission, we both went to get our coats, signaling that we wanted to step out for some fresh air. There was no objection from the coat check man. Outside, Luke and

"Let's split up," I gasped. "Give 'em two trails to follow. We'll meet at the tram stop."

"Okay," Luke agreed and broke across the darkened street like a wide receiver going for the long bomb. I ducked into the next alley and waited.

I didn't have time to explain to Luke what I intended to do, much less ask for his approval. If we were being chased, I had to neutralize the dog. If it had been unleashed, it would be well out in front of its master and I would have to disable or kill it quickly in order to get away. If it were still on the leash with the master running with it, I would need surprise and an incredible amount of luck to neutralize both of them, especially since the policeman certainly would have a pistol out.

In the darkness of the alley, I pulled out my pocket knife and opened the biggest blade, holding it underhand with the sharp edge facing up. With my left hand I pulled out the tin of red pepper, pulled the plastic sprinkle cap off with my teeth, spilling some of the hot powder into my mouth and left eye in the process. "Idiot!" I cursed myself, as my eye began to water and lips burn. At least I hadn't sniffed any of it.

I listened in the darkness. Nothing.

If the dog, either with or without its master, appeared around the corner, I planned to let them have the pepper full in the face as the dog attacked, offer my arm to the bite and stab quickly and as deeply as I could under the dog's chin with the blade. Then I would have to deal with the master as swiftly and violently as possible.

Still I listened. Nothing but my pounding heart. My face burned.

If the dog ran right on by or followed Luke, I would have a shot at the master first as he followed. The pepper followed by a disabling blow of some kind would be enough. That would be the best that could happen if it came to a fight. When a master is wounded, the dog is torn between continuing the chase and staying with its owner. Luke and I could probably get away uninjured that way. If I had to fight the dog, I might have to explain teeth marks to the Intourist guide at the theater. Or a crushed forearm.

It was getting hard to see and the pain in my eye was excruciating. I needed water and quickly. Still I heard no sign of pursuit.

I waited another half a minute and decided that maybe we weren't being followed after all. Spilling the pepper on the ground behind me to mask my scent, I walked off quickly into the night toward the tram.

Near the tram was a park with a fountain. The fountain was not working, but there was a puddle of ice cold water in it, which was good enough for me. For about five minutes I rinsed and rerinsed my eye until the burning gradually subsided. The occasional passer-by must have taken me for a drunk who had gotten himself beat up because nobody stopped to ask what was wrong.

Luke was waiting at the tram stop. "Why didn't you go back to the theater without me?" I asked.

"We've got time and I didn't know what had happened to you," he said. "By the way, what *did* happen to you. You look awful."

"I got some pepper in my eye by accident," and I explained how I had planned to use it to foil the dog.

"Well, your eye is all swollen up and your clothes are wet," he commented.

"It'll pass," I said, hoping it would.

We got back to the theater in the middle of the last act. I decided to wait around outside in the cool night air hoping it would do my face good and hoping no one would notice in the darkness. By the time the performance was over, the swelling had pretty much disappeared although the redness was still there. If anyone noticed, nobody said anything.

I was hoping the Intourist guide wouldn't ask us what had happened to us or how we liked the ballet. As it turned out, the only thing she was interested in was returning the same number of bodies to the hotel as she had left with.

It was good to get to bed that night and my prayers were deeply laced with gratitude. I fell asleep wondering what a Soviet jail felt like.

The next day was to be the most critical of our entire trip. We had to not only drop off the money but try to find out about the status of the underground printing press as well. Both of these items converged on a single man, a pastor of Luke's acquaintance, who lived on the other side of Kiev. It would involve a ride on the subway and two on trams as well as a good deal of walking. We decided to get an early start in scouting out the place and planning the approach we would make that evening.

We plotted out our planned route by map in the hotel

room after breakfast. Luke thought it should take about a half an hour by the looks of it. We would be using public transportation that night because, as before, there would be an Intourist-sponsored event (a circus) and we would skip out low profile to make our contact.

We took the car and Luke drove us right to the place. There could be no mistakes this time. We would ideally want to arrive at dusk, after daylight was gone but before the street lights came on.

We spent the rest of the day visiting an ancient church, being accosted in the process by some black marketeers wanting to buy our jeans. It amazed me that while Luke and I could shake the Intourist guides so easily and presumably the police as well, the black marketeers could always spot us, follow us until it was safe, and address us in our native language.

Leaving an hour for supper and an hour to make our way to the contact's house, I stuffed the roll of rubles in my pocket and we left, bundled up against the crisp Ukrainian autumn. On the way out, we picked up our tickets for the circus from the Intourist desk and told them we'd find our own way there. To my surprise, they went for it and let us go without insisting that we go with the group! That would be one less hurdle we'd have to jump.

We had spotted what appeared to be a decent restaurant not far from the hotel and we went in to have supper. Unfortunately, it was crowded and the waiter sat us at a table with two slightly drunk Russian soldiers. They greeted us formally but watched us with suspicion as we spoke, not understanding our language. They offered us some vodka but we refused as politely as possible. That didn't go over too well but when you start drinking with Russians you don't stop until every drop is gone and there is no money to buy any more and usually somebody is passed out. I stupidly made things worse by offering to toast with water, an insult to any drinking man.

They tried to make polite conversation but Luke and I were playing like we didn't understand Russian. Finally, things just settled into an uncomfortable silence as we waited for our food. Then I noticed the insignia on the one fellow's uniform indicating that he was a medic. "You are a medic?" I asked, making the universal sign of the shot needle with my thumb and two fingers.

"Da. A vui?" (yes, and you?) he answered.

"Da!" I lied with a smile and reached over to shake hands. From there on, the conversation got friendly. The medic's buddy had studied a little German, and with that we learned about their home towns, their favorite sports and communicated that we were tourists from Holland. At one point, the young man said with a sad shake of the head, "Our countries..." and he made a gesture of two fists hitting each other. "But I..." and he waved a hand in negation.

He asked where we were going next. I told him Odessa, Kishenev, Romania, Hungary and then home. When I said Romania, he brightened.

"Romania? My brother is stationed in Romania! Maybe you could look him up and tell him hello from me?"

I said no, it wasn't a good idea. If I looked up his brother, it could get him in trouble. "They might think we are spies," I said.

"Vui?! Spioni?!" (You?! Spies?!) he shouted.

The whole restaurant fell silent as every head turned our way. I tried to calmly reassure him that we weren't spies and everything was okay. Finally, everyone went back to eating, our friend settled down and our food came.

We ate quickly and left. So much for keeping a low profile.

The first leg involved getting on a tram and riding for about a mile. Getting on, I soon learned that you should have a ticket and get it punched in the machine by the door. I had no idea where one purchased such tickets, but as Luke hadn't seemed to make it a matter of concern, I followed his lead and rode like everybody else. (Actually, most people carry a monthly pass, but for those who don't, they buy tickets as magazine stands, stores and various places, but I didn't know that then.)

It almost never happens, but this time there was a ticket-checker on the tram, a big, heavy and not-at-all-friendly woman. She asked to see our tickets. She addressed Luke first, who stared down his nose imperially at her, pretending to listen with disdain, but not understanding what she wanted. The only thing he could think of to answer her with was, "Eta fsyo?" meaning, "Is that all?" This, of course, enraged the lady, who began to rant and rave, demanding things neither of us understood (probably identity cards), and getting only repeated "eta fsyo's" in response. Mercifully, the tram stopped and Luke and I jumped off, which ended the whole embarrassing spectacle. Our low profile was really taking a beating.

We made our way to the Metro, or subway, station.

I was looking forward to this. I had heard that they were awesome feats of engineering, deep enough in the earth to survive an atomic blast and with enough room to contain most of the population of the city in an emergency.

This time, we checked out the ticket situation before entering. You had to put a small coin in the turnstile and then you could go through. No ticket involved.

We got in one of the fast moving lines and, being first, I dropped my kopeck in the slot. The turnstile clicked as I pushed through. Then Luke put his in and pushed. Instead of a friendly click, he got the ear-splitting whoop of an alarm! It must have been a wrong sized coin and he hurriedly fished through his pockets for another one while people turned their heads and those in line behind him tapped their feet impatiently. I began to wonder if Alan Funt was hiding about somewhere.

The escalator seemed to descend for hours, deeper than I had even imagined. It was an almost frightening feeling. When we finally arrived at the bottom, we found ourselves in a cavern with tracks entering and leaving at both ends. People stood in groups waiting for the next train which soon arrived.

We got on and rode without incident to our planned stop, rode the long escalator to the surface and began looking about for our next tram stop. But first, we bought some tickets at a nearby news stand.

When we finally arrived at the street our contact lived on, we had used over an hour and a half, and it was very dark. Luke was a little worried.

We strolled past the house, keeping an eye peeled for

any signs of police surveillance. We waited across the street in the dim light for a few minutes, and just as we were about to cross over and go in, a man wearing a long overcoat arrived. He walked right through the front gate, around the back, and into the house.

"Oh-oh. Trouble," I said softly to Luke. We didn't want any unnecessary encounters with strangers.

"No. That's him! Our contact!" Luke said. We were extremely fortunate in arriving when we did. Had we arrived as planned, we would have missed him.

We walked across the street, through the gate and around the back. With Luke in the lead, we stepped up on the old wooden porch and were met at the door before we could reach for the handle. It was an old woman dressed in the typical attire of a Ukrainian peasant. Just past her, our contact was taking off his coat and a flash of recognition came over his face as he spied Luke and me.

"Brothers!" he exclaimed in Ukrainian and rushed over to hug each of us, Luke first.

We were ushered into the kitchen, which is the most important room in any Eastern European's home, and seated at the table. A snack of pickled tomatoes and boiled eggs was brought along with sweet, hot tea. The ladies of the house, despite our invitation to join us, disappeared politely after laying the table. In that society, women and men do not mix as equals.

Our conversation was warm but superficial mostly due to the difficulty in communicating in Ukrainian. We began with how the Church was getting on by the grace of God and how there were new converts every month. Mostly, they were meeting in the forests secretly. The smiles began to fade, however, when I asked about any recent arrests.

"Yes, there have been arrests," he said.

"Many arrests?" I pressed.

"Yes," he nodded reluctantly.

"Why?" I asked, wanting to pull the truth out of him. He apparently did not want to speak much about the situation. His answer was prefaced by a profuse apology for anything he might say that might be construed as negative toward us as Westerners, and that he knew that we loved them and want earnestly to help the Underground Church in the Soviet Union, et cetera, et cetera, but…"

He paused after the "but" with his eyes downcast.

"The Swedish boys?" I coaxed.

"The Swedish boys," he affirmed. "There have been many, many arrests. The damage they did was immense, though in God's name we know they didn't mean to do it." He said something to one of the women in the next room and she appeared a few seconds later with a package.

In the package was a veritable treasure. Slowly, reverently, she unwrapped what looked like just a bundle of papers. As I looked more closely, I realized that it was a complete Bible, copied by hand on common notebook paper. I gasped in amazement. She smiled faintly, venturing only to say that she copies the Bible by hand every chance she gets to see a real one. This was the result of years of work.

Not only was there a hand-written Bible in the package, but among the papers was a list of names, over a hundred in all, of believers that had been arrested and were still being held in prison without charge. Having explained to us the meaning of the list, our contact simply sat in expectant silence. He wanted to know whether we would try to take the list out but didn't want to ask us directly or be so blunt as to point out the dangers if we were caught.

My Russian teacher had once told me that in Russian, what a person doesn't say is often more important than what he does. What our contact was saying by his silence was immensely important.

"We have a way to get this out to the West," said Luke, who was anxious to get back into the conversation.

The pastor's eyes said, "So did the Swedish boys."

Returning his gaze, I said, "We will not try to take the papers across the border, only the information. Even if we are caught, there will be nothing to lead the police to you. I can tell you nothing more, but we can get the information out."

He nodded his ascent.

I took the papers, folded them and tucked them away through a hole in the lining of my coat. Only a thorough search would reveal them.

Next, Luke steered the conversation to the printing press. The question was immediately met by an earnest suggestion to forget about the press. A few years ago it was a good idea, but now the police pressure was just too much. They would not be able to get the press into operation again in the near future. That was that.

At this point it seemed probably the right time to bring out the money. Reaching into my pocket, I said, "We have brought a gift from the churches in Holland," and produced

recite the entire Koran from memory and more than one science fiction fan who can quote any line from any episode of any Star Trek program ever broadcast.

The rest of our stay in the Soviet Union was rather unremarkable and even enjoyable in a few instances. I found Odessa to be a very pleasant city with an almost Mediterranean character to it. Kishenev, by contrast, was quite forgettable.

The day before we were to leave the U.S.S.R. we stayed in a city near the Romanian border and got up at 5:00 a.m. in order to be there early. We were anticipating the kind of long wait we had endured upon entering the country and wanted not only to leave as quickly and smoothly as possible, but to get all the way across Romania if we could. Alas, it was not to be.

The first thing that caught our attention as we arrived at the border station in the frigid, grey dawn was that the chief of the station, an Army major, and our female translator were already up and wide awake even though it was before six. Although they were very polite, there was a tension in the air that came through as an almost too friendly attitude toward us. Such was not characteristic of our dealings with the Russians up until then.

First, our translator, a woman of about thirty-five, took our documents for the official processing and said she wouldn't be long. We could wait in the building until the guards came to inspect our vehicle and belongings. We didn't see our papers again for over seven hours.

Soon, however, the guards appeared and motioned for

us to accompany them to the car. We opened everything and they methodically went through the passenger compartment, the trunk, every piece of our luggage, the engine and sounded the gas tank with a wire. It was a thoroughness hitherto unsurpassed in my experience and took them over an hour. Over the course of that inspection, we made some small attempts to be friendly, offering them gum and sweets, which they accepted discretely.

Finally, upon finishing their task, they closed everything up and reported to the station chief. There was some discussion and the team came back and started the inspection all over, this time with the officer in occasional attendance, making suggestions about other places to look. They pulled out the seats, poked through the upholstery with needles, took off the steering wheel, took apart various parts of the motor, deflated and inspected the spare tire and performed numerous other minor observations that they hadn't previously.

Our translator was present to convey the inspection team's instructions when they required our cooperation and she was noticeably ill at ease. We tried to make pleasant conversation but it was hard going. Several times she tried to point out that when they travel abroad, they have to go through similar customs formalities in the West (nonsense, of course), and begged our indulgence. I asked how many times she had been in the West. She hadn't been yet.

This second and more thorough inspection lasted over two hours. When they finished, it was past ten o'clock and we were getting a little hungry. We pulled out a bag of bread and sausage, offering some to the guards and translator, who refused. They did, however, insist on us eating within their eyesight and inspecting the contents of the lunch bag before we dug into it.

We were just finishing up when the KGB car arrived.

Officers of the KGB wear distinctive uniforms, but even without them, their importance and menace would be obvious from the behavior of those around them. When three captains and a major parked the car and got out, the air took on a distinct chill. The guards, who had thus far been amiable, became icily aloof. The station chief, whose rank was equal to that of the senior KGB man and who was on his home turf, took on a stiffer, more rigid posture. He greeted the newcomers formally, with just a hint of obsequiousness, and was met with cold formality. After a few remarks, he turned and pointed to us and the cold glare of their collective gazes froze our whole inspection team, including the translator, solid. Someone was in big trouble.

And it looked like that "someone" was Luke and I.

One of the captains took immediate charge of the vehicle and luggage search and the team started in a third time on our car. One of the other captains gathered every piece of paper we had, including the trash. The remaining KGB captain and major disappeared into the building with the station chief.

I surmised that the officer in charge of the search was probably a specialist in counterintelligence while the one with the papers was a cryptoanalyst, a specialist in codes and clandestine communication. One or both of the others would have to be a specialist in interrogation. What four such important people were doing here just to see Luke and me I could only guess, but one thing for sure, it wasn't routine. They held us in grave suspicion of something.

Luke was noticeably more nervous, too, fidgeting and pacing. We had no evidence of any misdeed in our possession and our cover stories had been rehearsed and re-rehearsed. I still didn't feel we were in any particular danger yet. If we had been spotted doing anything in the country, they would have picked us up before now and indeed would not be trifling with our car. My best guess at the time was that they had some reason to believe that we were trying to smuggle something out of the country and that was one area in which our hands were clean.

As the translator tried to make light of the whole goings-on, as though it were routine and happened to every tourist who came through, I began to have a little fun.

"Are they perhaps looking for drugs?" I asked.

She shrugged and said, "It's possible. Young men your age could be carrying drugs out of the country."

"Is there much illegal drug traffic in the Soviet Union?" I asked.

"No! Is no drugs in Soviet Union!"

After a while, I remarked that they were very interested in our vehicle. Could it be possible that they thought we were trying to smuggle out weapons for terrorists?

"Yes. It is possible. Young men your age could be smuggling guns," she suggested.

"Is there much terrorism in the Soviet Union?" I asked.

"No! Is no terrorism in Soviet Union!"

Just a slave to temptation, a few minutes later I continued,

"I know! They have taken away all our papers, magazines and books. Perhaps they are looking for pornography."

"Yes. It is possible. Young men your age could be carrying pornography," she admitted.

"Is there much pornography in the Soviet Union?" I asked.

"No! Is no pornography in Soviet Union!"

The fruitless search of the car continued. This time they were unscrewing, unbolting and unfastening everything possible. I have never seen either trained mechanics or street hoods strip a car so expertly in such quick order. I wondered how in the world we were going to get it back together in any kind of shape to drive home.

Then, with a shiver, I realized that maybe they know we aren't going to be driving home any time soon.

Amazingly, they never recognized the secret compartment in the car for what it was. It looked like a piece of steel plate on the floor protecting the drive shaft and the hollow space between the floor and the differential looked like it belonged there. Of course, if there had been anything in it, it would have been found.

Before the vehicle search ended, the KGB man and the station chief came out and said something to the translator who told us that we must come inside for questioning. Only routine. But the look on both the officers' faces told me it was going to be anything but routine.

In the short walk to the building, Luke began frantically to remind me of our cover story. "We are just student tourists. We don't know anybody in the Soviet Union. We are only here to..."

"I know, I know. Take it easy. Everything will be all right," I tried to reassure him. Upon entering the building, they immediately separated the two of us and warned us not to talk to each other. To a trained interrogator, this act has a special significance.

When prisoners are taken, the so-called "Five 'S's" are observed: silence, segregate, search, safeguard, and speed to the rear. The shock of capture has to be preserved and the opportunity to get organized and destroy valuable intelligence on the prisoner must be prevented. Keeping us separated and quiet was the first indication that, technically, we were under arrest.

A room had been prepared for us and Luke was taken in first under strenuous protest. His nervousness had incubated into panic and he was loudly threatening to notify the embassy of this treatment until the slam of the door cut his protestations off from my hearing. I was left alone with my thoughts under the watchful eye of a young guard with a Kalashnikov.

I knew we were about to be interrogated and Luke's rising hysteria was a bad sign. Still, I was looking forward to the questioning in a perverse sort of way. I knew their techniques and, while they might rough us up a bit, I didn't believe that they would go so far as to physically injure us. We were, after all, American citizens and no matter what they thought we were up to, resorting to torture would be bad publicity. The Russians do not consider a little beating, however, to be torture.

It would be ineffective. I can take pain. Mentally I prepared myself.

The Russian guard noticed the subconscious smile on my face and, misinterpreting it as an attempt to be friendly, smiled briefly and turned his head away.

Several minutes later, Luke re-emerged, accompanied by two guards who escorted him at arms length to the toilet. Luke had developed a bad case of diarrhea which interrupted his session with the interrogators.

A few minutes later, it was my turn.

The translator told me that I should accompany her into the room. The cubicle was small but contained a guard, the two KGB men I suspected to be interrogators, the station chief, and the translator. There was a table at one side of the room with what looked like an airport x-ray machine on it. There was a solitary chair opposite the table behind which stood the guard, his weapon slung across his back and his gloved hands free. The chair was covered with a white linen bed sheet. Apparently, they did not want the prisoner to see how the chair was rigged.

Before seating me, the KGB captain knelt down to arrange the chair. As his hand with a ringed finger moved close to the seat, a buzzer sounded. There was a metal detector underneath, the purpose of which must have been to detect anything metal hidden in the detainee's pelvic cavities. The next step of the process came as no surprise. I was strip searched.

They took each article of my clothing, piece by piece and examined it thoroughly, and then placed it on the table to be scanned by the x-ray machine. When I was completely naked, despite the cold and the presence of a woman, the KGB man forced a gloved finger into my rectum. It dawned on me why they had seen fit to interrupt Luke's inquisition so abruptly. Perhaps that also explained the linen over the chair. It certainly explained why Luke's guards had held onto him so gingerly at arm's length.

I was then seated in the chair while the senior KGB man began the questioning through the interpreter. The opening questions were routine: Why was I visiting the Soviet Union? What had I seen? Where had I gone? Then the questions began to get more pointed:

"Who did you see while you were here?"

"Just other tourists, Intourist people, and occasional accidental acquaintances."

"What friends and relatives do you have in the Soviet Union?"

"None."

"What did you bring in with you of value?"

"Only what is listed on the entry forms we filled out."

The stream of questions was interrupted by the captain operating the x-ray machine. He had gotten to my shoes and the one with the secret compartment showed up on the screen. He traced the outline of the compartment in the sole of the shoe to the other two officers.

I felt my heart start to beat faster despite my attempts to will myself into calm. The KGB interrogator noticed my agitation, too. With a smug smile on his face, he walked over to me slowly, with a gesture dismissed the translator, and addressed me directly in Russian:

"Shto eta, takoye?" (Roughly: Well, now. What have we here?) he remarked, holding up the shoe.

"Nichevo," I responded, stupidly answering him in Russian. Nothing.

The backhand slap that followed took me completely by surprise. My head jerked to the side and I tasted my own blood at the corner of my mouth. For a few moments, I saw stars. He leaned in a couple of inches from my face.

"Deutsch, bitte, Deutsch."

I started to laugh in spite of myself. Something about the whole situation, me freezing my bare buns off in a Russian interrogation room and playing right into their hands despite my preparation, suddenly hit me as hilariously funny.

My interrogator, however, didn't register any hint of amusement. He leaned closer and asked again, "What is in the shoe?"

"Nothing," I said, and tucked my chin in in anticipation of the blow I expected.

"Nothing," he repeated. The unsaid "You expect me to believe that?" came through in the intonation.

"Open it," I suggested.

"I know there is nothing in the shoe," he responded. "What *was* in the shoe?"

"Money," I answered truthfully.

"Ah!" he exclaimed, his face brightening into an exaggerated smile. "Money. How much money?"

"I travel a lot and try to keep a couple of hundred dollars there for emergencies," I explained, reverting to English and keeping with my planned cover story. "But I used it all up by the end of August. It has been empty ever since. Go ahead. Open it if you like."

"You brought no extra money into the country with you?" he asked. "No foreign currency?"

"None," I answered. Strictly speaking, that was true.

"I wish I could believe you," he said, again the unsaid "but I don't" being the main idea communicated. "What about your friend?"

"He knows nothing about it. In fact, we only met just recently and decided to travel a little together. I don't completely trust him," I said, again for the most part true.

"You shouldn't," the interrogator remarked. "He's going to get you into trouble." This time the message was, "Come clean and tell me everything and we'll let you go. Your friend is the one in trouble." I didn't fall for it.

"I really don't know him very well," was my only response. After a silence, he said, "Get dressed. You understand I'll have to open this shoe in any case."

"No problem," I said, pulling on my clothes. When I finished, he motioned me out.

On the way out I passed Luke being escorted in. I tried to stop him for a few words, but the guards kept us apart. "Jig's up," I only managed to say with a wave as though it were a greeting. No comprehension registered on his face.

The young guard seated me where I had been before. "End of round one." I muttered to myself. Trying my best to accurately assess my situation, it seemed that they now knew that I had a secret compartment and that I spoke Russian to some degree. They had obviously been in communication with the Intourist agent who had pretended only to understand German when we entered, although perhaps my interrogator had only read his report or talked to him on the phone. It was a distinct possibility that my being cute with the "Deutsch, bitte" trick had resulted in the guy recommending that we be taught a little respect on the way out of the country.

So far they seemed more interested in the possibility that we were involved in the black market than in the Underground Church. If I could take the rap for being a petty hard currency smuggler, it would be acceptable in that it would keep our contacts out of trouble. I decided to stay with the money in the shoe story, admitting to bringing in a roll of rubles if it came to that. What did I spend it on, since I had nothing to show for it? The only believable answers I could come up with were girls or that I was robbed. Perhaps both would be even more believable. If I were robbed, I got off remarkable unscathed, but a prostitute could clean a drunk tourist out of his cash easily.

But if it did come out that we were believers working with the Underground Church, the prostitute story would be very bad. I decided to just say I had been robbed and got off lucky if it came to that.

It looked like it might come to that, too, if they really went to work on Luke. He was already in a very uncomfortable physical and mental state. He didn't know how much they had on me, either, and the ploy that a partner had turned traitor had worked on the Swedish boys. I sat and prayed that Luke would keep his head.

I stayed outside the interrogation room alone for over a half hour. The shock of being stripped and struck across the face had worn off and I felt ready for round two. I assumed they would get something out of Luke. In fact, they probably had a file on him already from his other trips. The "getting me into trouble" remark certainly suggested that they might have some dirt on Luke.

The door swung open and Luke was escorted out, full of wrath and indignation, claiming to personally know Jimmy Carter, who would sure as anything hear about this. They sat him down next to me and the officers went off alone to confer. That surprised me, letting us be together and talk.

"What did they do with you?" I asked.

"Asked all kind of crazy questions about black market contacts," he answered. "They said they knew you had a lot of money hidden in your shoe. Did you tell them that?"

"No," I said. "They found the secret compartment with the x-ray machine and I told them that sometimes I keep money in it for emergencies."

"Why did you tell them that?" he asked, showing his irritation. "You should have told them it was for something else."

"Like what? Religious tracts?" I jabbed.

"Of course not! But now they can get us for black marketeering because you told them you brought in a bunch of money," he said, his voice edged in anger.

"You don't know anything about the secret compartment or the money, remember?" I reminded him. "Just stay with your cover story and don't believe anything they tell you about me. We'll be okay. And if we have to spend some time in jail for black marketeering, it beats getting our friends thrown in with us, doesn't it?"

That calmed him down a little.

"We'll be okay," I reassured him. "Let the peace of God rule in your heart."

We fell silent for a while. I tried to get a little conversation going in a friendlier direction by asking, "How are you doing?"

"A little case of the runs, that's all," he said. "Embarrassing as shit."

I stifled a snicker. "Well, hang in there. We're going to be okay. You'll see."

After about a half an hour, the two majors returned with our translator and a couple of sheets of paper in their hands. The attitude of the translator was one of tangible relief. The station chief exhibited something of an apologetic posture while the KGB man remained stern. Clearly, he didn't approve of what was taking place.

"Would you sign these papers, please?" translated the woman for the station chief.

"Not on your life!" Luke refused with his arms crossed across his chest.

"What do they say?" I asked.

"Only that you suffered no mistreatment or loss of property while here," said the translator. "As soon as you sign them, you are free to go."

I suggested to Luke that we sign the papers and leave. We were getting off extremely lucky for some reason.

I signed my paper eagerly while Luke seemed to take his own sweet time. Finally, he assented and when he handed the paper back to the KGB man, he responded with a, "Spasiba, *Gospodin* Hanson." (Thank you, *Mister* Hanson.), "gospodin" being a form of address viewed with contempt as a relic of old Russia and being properly replaced by "tavarishch" (comrade).

To this day, I am not quite sure why they let us go. The KGB man certainly had enough reason to keep us a little longer. Perhaps he was overruled by some superior on the phone. Perhaps the ante was just too high. He had, after all, struck an American tourist and had no evidence to show anyone that we had done anything illegal at all. There would have been a stink if we actually turned out to be just a couple of innocent tourists. In any case, within a few minutes we were at the Romanian check point and within a half an hour, driving through Romania.

It was already afternoon and we wanted to drive hard to get as far as we could. I couldn't help but be struck by how beautiful Romania looked after the Soviet Union. By contrast Romania seemed so dismal entering from the colorful Hungarian side. We drove on and on until the sun began to set and we were still hours from the Hungarian border. We decided to overnight in a little campground, renting a bungalow for what amounted to pennies.

We slept poorly due to the lack of sleeping bags and mattresses. It was cold and there was no hot water either for showers or for cooking. Nevertheless, I couldn't help but view the morning with gratitude and optimism. An old peasant came around selling Transylvanian hand-embroidered table cloths. I already had one from my previous trip, but Luke wanted one and bought a nice purple and white specimen, although at too high a price.

That day we cleared both Romania and Hungary,

regrettably not staying in my favorite town of Debrecen that time. We did spend a pleasant night in Austria at a place with hot water and good food, however.

The pleasant trip home was marred only by a conversation we had in the car in which Luke pointedly asked me whether I had ever been baptized in the Spirit. My theology at that point was was firm that every believer is baptized in the Holy Spirit at the point of salvation and I said as much. Luke took issue with that, insisting that the event was an optional, post salvation experience and that no believer was fit for service without it. We broke off the conversation before it got too heated. I was growing intolerant of Charismatics at that point in my spiritual development and Luke considered the issue to be crucial to the success, or more correctly, the reason for the failure, of any mission into Communist territory. Although I didn't see it for months, in his report to the mission Luke unequivocally laid the blame for the problems we faced on the trip on my being unbaptized and recommended that people not baptized in the Holy Spirit be not allowed to participate in assignments of such importance in the future.

I reconstructed from memory the list of jailed Russian dissidents and turned it over to Amnesty International, just as we had done with the Czechoslovak list a month before. My report on the status of the printing press and the damage done by the Swedish boys was submitted and filed, where it stayed untouched for as long as I remained on staff. In the report I carefully pointed out that these were examples that, if poorly planned, our efforts were often not only unfruitful, but counterproductive with potentially disastrous consequences for those we intended to help. The printing press project had been plagued from the start by misunderstanding due to the mission never sending in anyone who spoke the language well enough. The Swedish boys incident spoke for itself. If we weren't more careful in the future, these disasters would only keep on happening.

Working with Luke also caused me to think again about working with Charismatics. Although some were clearly unstable and even psychotic to the point of hallucinations, Luke was not. He believed things that were internally consistent within his belief system but how did he stay in that belief system when reality clearly showed it to be faulty? How could he continue to search blindly for a house when we had the map right there in our possession? He would have had to admit that his faith in the promise of success from God wasn't working. Resorting to the map would have been surrender to rationality, the enemy of faith. He reacted by flipping out in tongues.

I came to understand that speaking in tongues was the perfect tool for blocking rational thought when it threatened one's faith. Since rational thought is consciously processed through our internal dialog, through words, blocking that system by babbling incoherently effectively stops the intrusion of reason into the belief system. It probably works for any belief system that incorporates ritual chanting in languages the chanter does not comprehend like Latin, Hebrew, Arabic or Sanskrit. If the mission favored these people over those who rely on thoughtful consideration, could we really expect success?

I began to consider that perhaps the time had come for me to move on.

A NIGHT AT DRACULA'S

The mission was a fascinating mix of people from many places and backgrounds. English was the common language used at the Farm but comprehending a language was not the same as understanding a person. The two main mechanics, Alistaire and Jean Pierre, provided a microcosm that precisely illustrated the difference. Alistaire was a Scotsman whose English was entirely incomprehensible, yet his meaning was always clear. Jean Pierre, on the other hand, spoke English very well, yet his intentions and opinions were opaque.

While Alistaire had a brooding, dour personality, Jean Pierre was the kind of guy you couldn't help but like. A Frenchman educated at a Bible school in Switzerland, he was unusual among us. Evangelical Frenchmen are very rare birds. What was more, he was very easy going, always seemed to be in a good mood, tolerant, and never had a bad word to say about anybody. In fact, he seemed to keep his opinions so much to himself that people often wondered just what Jean Pierre believed. He refused to be drawn into an argument, forced into making a decision affecting anyone else, or in any way influencing matters at the mission.

I first met Jean Pierre and Alistaire on my first summer

"Oui, Monsieur," I answered.

"Excuse me?" he said.

"I said yes I do," I explained. "Oui, Monsieur is French."

"Oh," said Jean Pierre.

"I want to practice my French while I'm with you, if you don't mind," I said, handing him another box to put in the trunk.

"I do not mind," he said. "Merci."

"De rien," I responded. After a short silence I asked, "Was that correct?"

"Yes, but I would not say that," Jean Pierre commented.

"Why not? That's what the books say is the correct response."

"It is correct, but no Frenchman would say that," he said.

"What would a Frenchman say for 'You're welcome'?" I pressed.

"It depends."

"Just for example," I pressed further.

"De rien," he said with a shrug.

I decided to drop the interrogation. Perhaps French is something you just have to absorb through the skin by ample exposure to French people. Or maybe French food.

"What kind of food do you like, Jean Pierre?"

"French food, of course."

"What is your favorite dish?"

"Anything is fine," he answered.

"Well, do you like escargot?"

"You mean snails? Of course, my friend. They are delicious. Do you also like?"

"I've never tried escargot," I admitted.

"Then we must find a French restaurant in the road and I will help you to try them on."

"Sounds good," I agreed.

We left Holland on the morning of the 28th of December and, instead of going straight into Germany through Aachen like we usually did, we swung south through Belgium in search of a French restaurant to have a lunch of escargot. Eventually we found a promising little establishment and entered. Sure enough, escargot was on the menu.

We ordered two plates, each with twelve little black slimies floating in the appropriate sauce. Jean Pierre closed his eyes in rapture enjoying the aroma of a real French meal.

"It is magnificent," he commented.

"C'est magnifique," I agreed.

"Pardon?" he asked.

"Never mind," I said. "Bon appetit."

"Bon appetit to you too, my friend," he returned.

"You understood me when I said 'Bon appétit.'" I said ruefully.

"Of course. It is English," he said and speared a snail with the proper fork.

I tried a snail. Don't ask me to describe the taste or texture. Suffice it to say that I ate one and Jean Pierre ate twenty-three.

We took a leisurely course through Germany, overnighting at Regensburg. The next day we pressed on through Austria and into Hungary. We stayed overnight in Debrecen, the guests of my favorite family. After a satisfying meal, a good night's rest and pleasant company, we left early to make Bucharest by evening.

It was a long haul, but as the day waned, we found ourselves approaching the outskirts of the Romanian capital. I drove while Jean Pierre navigated with the map.

"You could turn left here if you like," he suggested.

or: "The light is red. You can stop if you prefer."

and finally:

"That is the house on the left. If you wish to stop the car, I wouldn't mind."

We had to deliver some material which consisted of little more than a handful of computer manuals and some spare parts. At the same time, we hoped to pick up some information on the state of affairs in the unregistered churches. The house we were visiting was the home of a Baptist pastor of one of the largest churches in Romania. He himself was only there long enough to say hi and bye, having a service to conduct that evening. However, we left the stuff with him and stayed for dinner, Jean Pierre chatting happily with the man's teenage daughter, who spoke excellent French.

We weren't the only guests. There were two Romanian Saxons, members of the Brethren denomination, a church I had had previous dealings with. They of course spoke German. From them I was able to find out that they were doing fine and their congregations were stable, though small.

"Are there enough Bibles?" I asked, hinting at the forty thousand I had helped bring in a couple of months earlier.

"Yes, we have enough. There is always one available somewhere," he responded.

"Enough for your new converts, too?"

"There aren't many new converts. In our church most of us have grown up with the faith. It's not so interesting for a non-Saxon to look into our church. The other churches, like the Baptists," and he smiled at our hosts, "are more active in evangelizing. They even evangelize among the gypsies!"

"What about the Army of God?" I asked, referring to a much publicized movement among the Romanian Orthodox.

"We don't have much contact with them. It's mostly priests and old people."

"But I heard there were lots of young people involved," I objected.

"I wouldn't say so," he said in return. "But, as I said, we don't have much contact with them." After a thoughtful pause, he ventured, "I do know a person who could tell you more about it, though. He lives near Brasov, on your way home."

"How could we meet him?" I asked, my excitement growing.

"A friend of mine is leaving for Sigisoara tonight after the prayer meeting. He could take you there."

The prospect of making yet another contact after a long

camp deep in the Ukraine. He finally managed to escape and walked all the way back to Romania living off the land and the hospitality of the village peasants along the way. At the time I heard it, I remember having some doubt as to its veracity, but having lived in Hungary now for so many years, I have encountered similar stories among veterans. I suppose it was, at least in large measure, true.

Life in Romania in the 1950s and 60s was no picnic either. There were always shortages, the aftermath of a very devastating war and the top-to-bottom restructuring of society by the Communists. The worst years came with Ceaucescu, the self-proclaimed "Genius of the Carpathians," in the 1970s. His economic policy of selling the best of Romanian produce abroad and keeping the worst for his people made life difficult. Carried to the extremes he did, it became illegal to own or raise unregistered farm animals. The result was that people were raising chickens and pigs in their homes secretly and ratting each other out to the police. It became a crime to feed one's own family in that manner, and the hatred generated by a person who was low enough to report such a thing (either for a reward or to avoid being punished as an accomplice) to the police made for grudges that would be held for years. The effect was to set neighbor against neighbor at a time when cooperation was badly needed. It brought out the worst in people and perpetuated what is known as the "Balkan Mentality."

The Balkan Mentality is a xenophobic, reactionary attitude that resists change of any sort and lauds ethnic purity. All people outside one's own ethnic group are subject to suspicion if not open hostility, as the civil war in Yugoslavia aptly illustrated. The vision of the pogroms, the rampaging of Romanian miners through Hungarian villages, looting shops and beating to death with clubs anyone who didn't speak Romanian without an accent, still burns in my memory.

A large part of the country consists of Transylvania, which is ethnic Hungary and was given to Romania by the Allies as a reward for dropping out of the Second World War before Hungary did. Hungarians living in Hungary made great efforts to relieve the hardships faced by their relatives across the border. A foreigner could not stay overnight in a Romanian house, even with relatives. There was a period when gifts could not be accepted, even food or gasoline.

The efforts the police made to stop such practices ranged from heavy fines to prison sentences and occasionally making people disappear. There was one case of a friend of mine in Debrecen, originally from Transylvania, who stayed overnight with his parents on a visit home. A neighbor reported it and the parents were fined three months' wages. Another friend of mine, a doctor in Cluj, had been instrumental in getting people out of the country for medical treatment abroad. The organization that arranged for the treatment falsified some papers, and although my friend had no part in it, because he knew about it and didn't report it, he went to jail for three years. The perpetrators of the falsification, members of a missionary organization in California, were never prosecuted, of course. I doubt the U.S. government would even bother to investigate such a thing.

Worst of all, my friend with whom I was enjoying the conversation on the way to our new contact's house outside of Brasov, would disappear one day in a "traffic accident" leaving his young wife a widow and two children fatherless. The funeral was to be a closed casket affair because the body was so badly damaged, but the man's mother managed to get into the undertaker's office the evening before the burial and view the body. The undertaker had gone home and the night watchman didn't know it wasn't allowed. My friend's body had a neat bullet hole in the back of the skull and half the face was missing where the slug had exited on the left side.

All this would, of course, take place in the future. At the moment, I was happy to enjoy his company and fellowship. After a short introduction, my friend walked out of the door and out of my life forever to continue his journey home. Getting to the waiting car, he smiled and waved as the car moved off into the blackness of night.

Our contact, besides being a very interesting man, had some good information for us to bring back to Brother Piet whose ubiquitous hand I repeatedly discovered behind most of the important projects in Eastern Europe, especially Romania and Bulgaria. It was his opinion that the Army of God movement was overrated. Although probably not severely compromised by government infiltration, it was nevertheless ineffective. They mostly wanted to call people back to a medieval worship of icons and observation of tedious ritual. It just wasn't for our day and age.

The forty thousand Bibles delivered, on the other hand, had been an unqualified success. Their distribution had not only filled a great need for the literature, but had greatly inspired the local congregations.

"What else can we do?" I asked.

"Pastor study materials," was the immediate reply. "They need lexicons, dictionaries, concordances, systematic theologies."

It was a sentiment I had heard voiced before in other countries as well. The pastors need training and we could provide the tools to train them in some measure.

"Is there anything we could bring you personally the next time we come through?" I asked. He asked for a comb.

"Tell Piet that I would like one of those metal combs like he brought me. I lost the last one."

"You mean like this?" said Jean Pierre after I translated his request. He pulled out a small comb made of aluminum.

"Yes, that's it exactly," the old man said.

"But we only use these for dogs," objected Jean Pierre. I decided not to translate, but I could see that the old man knew enough English to understand because he laughed uproariously. Jean Pierre gave him the comb as "one dog to another" and assured him that he could find another in the Netherlands for himself.

"There are also dogs in Holland," my French friend noted.

It was past ten when we left. Neither of us was sure what we should do. We could press on all night, driving in shifts, but the more we drove, the more I felt that we should get a hotel room. After all, we needed and deserved the rest. And we weren't in any hurry.

The night was cloudy and an icy wind had come up. Driving in Transylvania at night is no fun anyway, but the stormy conditions in the dead of winter made things worse.

There had been no snow for weeks and the pavement was clear, but it was still unpleasant driving on the winding mountain roads with their occasional potholes and horse-drawn wagon swinging the customary lantern on the back eerily in the dark of the night.

We got to a little town named Bran and I broke the suggestion to Jean Pierre.

"Would you like to get a hotel for the night?"

"Anything is possible," he answered. I took that as a yes.

It was almost midnight when we woke up the clerk at the front desk of the biggest little hotel on the main street of town. We checked in fast, and in record time were both sawing logs.

We woke up to find almost two feet of snow on the streets. The wintry scene that greeted us through our upstairs window was one for a Christmas picture postcard, a sleepy Transylvanian town nestled in the forested mountains and blanketed with a thick covering of cotton-like whiteness. We were refreshed. English lacks an expression for being "slept out," meaning having slept as much as one needs, but that's what we were.

And we were hungry. So as soon as we'd finished our morning ablutions, we headed downstairs to the dining room, ready for whatever there might be to eat.

We found a table and a waitress brought us the customary continental breakfast. We were just starting in when I heard American English being spoken, rather loudly, across the room by a big, bald-headed gentleman who was trying in vain to explain that he wanted eggs, and over easy if possible. With ham. He was apparently of the opinion that English can be better understood when spoken loudly. Jean Pierre and I watched the spectacle with amusement for a few minutes and went back to eating and talking (quietly).

The gentleman, who didn't get his eggs or ham, finally resigned himself to eating whatever they served and the dining room resumed the pleasant hum of conversation over breakfast enjoyed by a dozen or so customers.

We were just finishing up when a young Romanian woman with dark hair and glasses came over to our table and said, in a perfect British accent, "Pahdon me, but ahr you English?"

"No. I'm American and my friend here is French," I answered.

"Oh, American! That's great," she said, switching accents to match my own. "How ya doin'? And what brings you to Bran? Skiing, maybe?"

"No. Actually, we're just passing through and got snowed in. And you? Do you live here?" I continued, surprised to find someone whose English was so good.

"No, I'm just on a vacation skiing. Mind if I sit down? I don't get much chance to practice my English anymore."

"By all means. I'd love some company," I said.

Jean Pierre, who had finished his breakfast, got up to leave saying, "If you'll permit my excuse, I think I'll return to the room and douche myself if you don't mind," and "Enchanted to have made your acquaintence," to the lady.

"So how did you learn to speak such good English?" I opened.

"I was a tour guide for a few years and had the chance to speak quite a bit. Now I'm just an English teacher in a high school in Bucharest," she said.

"And now you're here to do some skiing? I didn't know there was a ski resort in the area," I remarked.

"Oh, yes," she said. "Of course, it isn't as good as Switzerland, but it's much cheaper, and very nice all the same." She paused a moment thoughtfully, and then, with a look in my eyes held for just a fraction of a second too long said, "My doctor told me to take a vacation and do whatever I want. I hope you don't think me too bold to have come over here just like that."

"No, not at all," I reassured her.

"Well, I wanted to come over here and talk to you in English, and the doctor told me to do whatever...I...want... to...do." and she let the last few words hang in the air. "This has to be a set-up," I thought to myself.

"Well, it looks like we're both going to be stuck here for at least a day. Are you going skiing today?" I asked.

"No," she answered. "Because of the snow we can't get to the resort. Maybe I could show you around the town a little. I used to be a tour guide."

"I'd like that," I said. "Should we meet in the lobby in, say, half an hour?"

"No," she said. "Let's meet outside on the street instead. But in an hour, okay?"

"Okay," I agreed.

After she left, I noticed that the only one left in the dining room was the American gentleman. He looked my way and, with a wave and a smile said, "Hi. American, too?"

I said, "Yeah."

"You're here to see the castle, of course," he remarked.

"No. I just got snowed in by accident on my way back from Bucharest. What castle?" I asked.

"Why, Dracula's castle! It's the only thing of any importance in this area," he said. "I'm here on sabbatical to study the historical Dracula," and he went on to explain how he was a professor from Boston University and had been in Romania for several months tracking down records on the notorious Vlad Tepis, or Vlad the Impaler.

When we finished our coffee, he invited me up to his room to see some of his research. It was extremely interesting, but I had an appointment to keep and excused myself, promising to return later.

I meant to tell Jean Pierre that I would be out for most of the day, but he had already left to go out for a walk, so I just quickly brushed my teeth, got my coat, cap and gloves, and made my way downstairs.

In the lobby sat one of the most obvious plain-clothes policemen I have ever seen. Traveling as much as I have in the East, I was used to being followed, but nowhere were they more blatant than in Romania. I think that often they try to appear obvious just to intimidate foreigners. This fellow was sitting in a chair, holding up a newspaper, and watching people come and go. It then occurred to me why my "tour guide" preferred to meet me outside instead of here in the lobby. She had probably noticed the cop. That

get divorced the next day easily in Paris or Las Vegas. I'd pay you anything I can..."

I stood in stunned silence, feeling both remorse and pity for her.

"I... I can't..." I could only say. How could I explain to her what such an act would do to my work as a Bible smuggler?

"I'll get a job and pay you a little each month for as long as I live," she went on.

"It's not the money," I said. "It would ruin my work."

She turned away and sniffled a little, not just from the cold. I reached for a handkerchief to dry her eyes.

"Believe me, I want to help you, but I'm trying to help a whole lot of Romanians. Getting you out of the country in this way would put a stop to all that," I started, and then caught myself. I shouldn't have even said that much. "Come on," I said, putting my arm around her shoulder, "Let's see the rest of the castle."

After a while, she got a grip on herself and tried gamely to return to the friendly banter we had been enjoying up to that point. We eventually found ourselves on one of the top floors in what had to be the master bedroom. There was a huge bed with four massive spiraling wooden posts and a headboard of solid oak carved into a scene of wild animals. The centerpiece of the scene was a wolf's head, the tongue hanging out grotesquely. Certainly only Dracula could have slept peacefully under that sight!

In the felt slippers, our feet were cold, and my friend suggested we warm them up a bit.

"How? By lighting a fire?" I asked.

"No. Like this," and she pulled back the thick embroidered velvet bedspread and hopped into Dracula's bed. "Come on!" she said pulling off her slippers and playfully patting the mattress. I climbed up and sat on the bed in front of her. She took my feet in her hands and rubbed.

I did the same.

It did warm my feet up, I must admit. It began to warm up more than my feet, too. As she rubbed my one foot with her hand, she rubbed the other between her thighs. Occasionally, she squeezed extra hard with her thighs, pushing her pubic bone against my sole and, half closing her eyes, began to let out little moans of pleasure.

After a few minutes of that, she grabbed the bedspread and, pushing me back gently, pulled it over us both as we lay down together. It felt ridiculous, lying together in Dracula's bed, wrapped up in winter clothes including the overcoats and hats, but at least it was warm and cozy. We snuggled a bit and it felt good. Then we kissed. Making love was out of the question, if only because of the cold, but we stirred each others' passions none the less.

At least I thought making love was out of the question. She had other ideas.

"We should be starting back. It's getting near lunch time," she said. "Are you ready to, uh, finish?" She didn't know the proper American expression for what she intended to do to me. After rejecting her proposal, I hadn't expected the matter to go any further, but this new friend in Dracula's bed displayed an honest consideration for my needs. She had gotten me excited and as a matter of course felt it was her responsibility to get me unexcited. She may also have been trying to show me that being my wife, if even for a short time, would not be unpleasant.

In the freezing cold master bedroom of Dracula's castle, aided by my sympathy for her and her predicament, I found this girl's offer to please me something precious, an obligation of honor that would be insulting to turn down.

But I did.

We lay in bed for a while in silence and then slowly, reluctantly departed, saying good-bye to Dracula after collecting our boots at the door.

Back at the hotel, I spent most of the rest of the day in the company of the professor from Boston listening to him in rapt fascination as he expounded on his favorite subject, Vlad the Impaler. As we got to be better friends, he began to confide in me that he had made some good friends while in Romania and was looking for a way to at least get a couple of college-age kids out to America to study. He warned me solemnly not to try to make friends with the Romanians if I could help it. The police pick them up and occasionally beat them just for talking to foreigners. He personally knew of several cases.

I didn't let on that I was well aware of that along with the informer networks and the death squads of the Securitate, the Romanian secret police. It was one more incident on top of that morning's that put even more steel into my spine to do something to bring down the whole damned system.

A TIME FOR GOODBYES

When we got back to Holland, Millie informed me that Paul wanted to talk to me. It seemed that my support was not coming in and something had to be done. It was an old problem that had dogged me from the outset. Before leaving America, the three of us, Paul, my pastor and I, had agreed that the church would send a thousand dollars each month for the twelve months I was to work in Holland as well as pay my round trip air fare. At the end of the year, we would reconsider where to go from there. Of the $1,000 a month the church agreed to send, the mission would keep half and I would get the other half. From my half I would pay the mission for my room and board, which left me $250 a month for my personal needs. Since that was a very small amount, I was free to raise extra support and the church would send it along to me with their $1,000 monthly commitment.

I had been at the mission for over six months and no money had arrived yet, despite several letters from the pastor and phone contacts through my family assuring me that it would. It was just an administrative oversight.

Six months is a long time for an administrative oversight to go uncorrected, so I didn't blame Paul in the least for being concerned. I was also a little uneasy because of the occasional letters I got from people in the church and relatives asking whether I had gotten the money they were sending. Until then the sum total of money I received from America was the $2 bill in a letter from little Lisa Kaiser I mentioned several chapters ago.

I was living pretty much off my savings for college and student loans I would have to pay back and was down to the point where something had to happen or I would be once again stranded overseas.

I had a suggestion.

"Paul, it's the middle of winter and we aren't doing much in the East anyway. Why don't you let me go home for a couple of months. I can get the support problem straightened out and at the same time work up a pastors' library project."

For a couple of months I had been pestering the mission to find pastor study materials to meet the number one request of ministers in the East. Paul had always maintained that this was not a mission of development but one of delivery. In other words, we don't decide what the believers should get; we just deliver what is available. I found that unsatisfactory. I already knew where to get pastor study materials that would suit our requirements and felt pretty sure that I could get funding for it, too.

"That might be a good idea. Let me think about it and talk it over with the others. I'll let you know what we decide soon," he said.

It was on the next Monday that Paul called me into his office. I felt sure that this would be a creative solution to everybody's concerns and was in a bright and optimistic mood.

"Well, Lloyd, we've decided to let you go. You can go back as soon as you can get a ticket. We also think it would be best if you just stayed home, too, and not come back."

My stunned silence was all I could give in response. After a few uncomfortable seconds Paul continued, "I've talked to everyone. They all agree that you are just not part of the team. Maybe if you go back and work in the church for a year or two, after that you will be ready to work on a mission again."

That deflated my mood. I should have felt angry, I suppose, but by that time I had already lost whatever respect I ever had for Paul or the mission. The emotion that registered most prominently was pity. "Alright. If that's the way it is, that's the way it is," I said. Paul stood, shook my hand and showed me out of his office. It had been hard for him, I know. He doesn't like confrontation.

Throughout the day the staff avoided my gaze. Everyone knew I had gotten the sack. I knew Paul hadn't talked to everyone like he said, but it didn't matter. What he said was basically true. I didn't fit in. This wasn't the place for me.

I just couldn't get into the long, rambling, fervent prayers; mine were generally short and to the point. They read the Bible to reinforce what they already believed to be true; I studied to learn new things. They were spiritual; I was worldly. They were chaste and I was weak. I had never learned to hide my appreciation for a fine wine and art. I couldn't bring myself to demonstrate a proper contempt for the flesh. I listened to non-Christian music. I drew non-Christian pictures. I read non-Christian books. And lately I had begun to associate with non-Christian Dutch neighbors.

Paul was right. I really didn't fit in.

I met Jan Vanderwald long enough to say good-bye. I hoped to leave on a friendly note, at least. About as friendly as it got, however, was his honest comment that he had always been against my employment from the start.

"I knew you would never work out," he said.

At least it turned out to be incorrect to say that the entire mission felt the same. Joop was genuinely sorry to see me go. He himself would leave in frustration within the year. As I collected the information I would need on pastor study material requests, he showed me how he had been computerizing the records and gave me a floppy disk of all the mission reports he had compiled so far.

Brother Piet, who had treated me fairly if severely, had hopes of turning me into a top-notch agent someday. I always accepted his criticism gratefully and with respect, as a pupil should from his master. He was one of the best in our business and it was a distinct honor that he granted me so much attention. When he heard I was leaving, he made a point of seeing me and suggesting that I consider working for another organization, a secular organization. It shouldn't have surprised me that Piet was into deeper things than a petty Bible smuggling operation.

Dave and Ruth were also gone for good. I would meet them a few months later in California on my search for pastor study materials where they shared with me their misgivings. Dave had been particularly concerned about how the need to raise money diverted the mission from meeting the true needs of the Underground Church and led it into compromises that actually hurt the believers we were trying to help.

There was another personality, Dr. Truax, a physician who had carried quite a lot of Bibles into the East over the years. He was to be a great comfort to me in those dark days as I struggled to get life and economic situation back under control. He loaned me a car and provided no small amount of financial support. Best of all, he kept me informed as to the activities of the mission after I left. Although Paul had said he would keep in touch, I never heard from them directly ever again, except when he came to America a few months later on a fund raising trip.

Paul was to meet with my pastor and try to get the several thousand dollars he had expected to receive in connection with my support. I wasn't supposed to be there, but Dr. Truax and his wife arranged to get the three of us together in their home and helped mediate a very uncomfortable situation.

For the seven months I was in Holland, my pastor had assured me by letter several times that the support was there and would be coming soon. When I saw him in person, his story changed. His understanding was that I would be allowed to raise support from within the church and the church would send it over. No money had come in, so no money was sent. This little piece of dishonesty was made all the more loathsome in that several people in the church had informed me of the money they had donated specifically for my support.

Paul presented the pastor with a two-page letter outlining all my violations of mission policy which were the basis for my dismissal. Of course, that was news to me. Paul had never mentioned any issue of violations of policy. In fact, the whole letter smelled fishy. Not only were most of the items completely without basis in fact, they were mostly things Paul could have had no direct knowledge of.

For example, it was alleged that I couldn't speak Bulgarian well. How would Paul be in a position to judge that? Or anyone at the mission for that matter? I was pretty sure that Jan Vanderwald was behind the letter.

"Paul, I know you didn't write that letter," I said. "Where did you get all that nonsense?"

"Lloyd, the staff discussed your involvement in the mission. These are matters everyone is aware of."

"Everyone but me, it would seem. Why didn't you ever say anything to me before? If I violated mission policy, you should have called me in on the spot to correct the matter. How is it that now is the first time I hear about it?"

Paul turned to the other two and lied to them in my presence that he had discussed these problems with me, but since I continued to violate policy, to be a "mission within a mission," as he put it, they had to let me go.

He couldn't meet my eyes and I could only shake my head in disbelief.

The conversation then turned to the matter of the money the church had promised. "This should be interesting," I thought to myself. To my astonishment, the pastor immediately agreed to deliver a check for the full amount without any discussion. The mission got its pledged amount and I got nothing, not even my agreed share, much less the airfare that also came out of my own pocket.

The financial harm to me was substantial. I had paid for my upkeep out of student loan money which I had to pay back. That forced upon me the decision of whether or not to sue the church or drop the matter. It was probably the wrong move, but I chose to drop it. Christians suing Christians always looks bad. I told myself that God would see that justice would be done, but it was just an excuse to avoid my responsibility of enforcing the contract. I deserved the financial hardship I eventually suffered. My responsibility went beyond my own right to the promised support. I had obligations to repay student loans and was therefore obligated to enforce the contract to be able to do it.

It also eventually came to light that this particular pastor had a history of shaddy financial dealings. My case was only one instance. I also had a moral obligation to do what I could to put a stop to it. Instead, I walked away.

So here were two major moral failures in my life not even remotely counterbalanced by resisting the temptation of two great opportunities for sex I still kick myself for missing. But let's add another:

I probably never would have had the spine to break with religion had not I been the victim of something this foul. I always knew that Christians are no better than unbelievers, as the bumper sticker says "not perfect, just forgiven." But the ease with which lying and deceit came to Paul and my pastor shocked me. It was as if they knew God was not watching. I also knew I should dissociate myself from Charismatics; I just couldn't bring myself to separate from the tongues-healings-prophesy crowd despite the obvious instability. Too many of my dear friends were in it. Though it is hard to be proud of being a Christian these days, I loved my faith. Now at least I can stop turning a blind eye to the misdeeds of so many who use religion to control others and excuse themselves.

When you know the truth, it really does set you free.

POSTSCRIPT

No one from my church or mission ever attempted to contact me after I left, nor did I them. It was a clean and painful break but it healed quickly. I lived to see my pastor study materials taken into the East and eventually even to be produced there long after the mission collapsed. The Transylvanian pastors who got the material and began to use ICE methodology became know as "Tematistak" or "Themists," a word play on Colonel Thieme's name and his method of teaching by categories or themes. Orderly, systematic study and teaching left their mark on the right group of believers at the right time in history.

I called Piet and found more fulfilling work, eventually moving to Hungary and playing a small personal role in the overthrow of Communism when at last its end came in 1989. That was a privilege beyond price.

Most precious was the freedom I felt when I left religion behind. It had been a life of obligatory hypocrisy, spurning all natural joys to maintain a façade of holiness. My American church was hollow. I watched it swell to thousands like other megachurches by becoming more like the enterainment-centered American culture until Sunday morning services resemble a performance, complete with program and credits.

Meanwhile my tiny adopted church in Eastern Europe stood up before tanks and machineguns. In the winter of 1989 we marched arm in arm, candles in hand dripping wax that I would never remove onto my shoes, singing the forbidden *Sarga Rozsa* (Yellow Rose) and daring armed soldiers to shoot us. The wall came down. Communism collapsed.

That was real and I was there.